500

TIPS

on

ASSESSMENT

500
TIPS
on
ASSESSMENT

Sally Brown,
Phil Race
&
Brenda Smith

Crest Publishing House

(A JAICO ENTERPRISE)
G-2, 16 Ansari Road, Darya Ganj
New Delhi-110 002

Published by :
KOGAN PAGE INDIA PVT. LTD.
(For Crest Publishing House)
2/13 Ansari Road,
Darya Ganj, New Delhi-110002.

500 TIPS ON ASSESSMENT
ISBN 81-242-0415-2

First Indian Edition : 2004

Printed by :
Efficient Offset Printers
215, Shahzada Bagh Industrial Complex
Phase-II, Delhi-110035.

Contents

Preface and Acknowledgements

Assessment of students' work, we believe, causes teachers in higher and further education more difficulties than any other area of their professional work. Growing numbers of students, coupled with severe financial restraints, have led to a struggle to maintain existing standards, let alone attempt to improve quality in ways required of us by both funding bodies and the sharpening expectations of students themselves. At all levels, quality assessors are seeking to discover whether our assessment systems are fair, valid, reliable, efficient and effective. We need to ask ourselves whether our systems assess not only what is taught, but what is learned. Do we measure skills and the ways in which these can be translated to other contexts? Do our systems provide a reasonable workload for students and staff alike? Are our systems effective, efficient and manageable, or do they drive us to despair? Can the students get easy access to the information about their work that helps them to improve?

Not only do we need to be achieving all these aims, but we also need to be able to demonstrate to all concerned that we are doing so. Added to this, there are increasing pressures upon us to assess both what students know and what they are capable of doing with such knowledge. This becomes made the more urgent with the emphasis on competence-based assessment through, for example, the National Council for Vocational Qualifications (NCVQ) in England and Wales, and similar agencies elsewhere. If we want students to learn well, we must match our assessment processes accordingly.

How we assess our students has a profound effect on what they learn, and on the ways in which they learn. If our choices of assessment strategies provide systems under which students are goaded into activities that privilege short term memory, information recall and surface learning, we should not be surprised if the outcomes are exceedingly poor in terms of learning gain.

In this book, we aim to provide hard-pressed lecturers in higher and further education with some practical guidance on how to tackle the key issues in assessment. It should not be seen as a recipe book on how to get assessment right, but rather as a menu of ideas from which to choose those approaches most suitable for the particular working environments each lecturer encounters.

We have grouped (well over) 500 tips into ten main chapter areas to help you find the parts of the book of most relevance and value to you. Inevitably, there is some overlap between the sections, as the areas we cover are often interdependent. What we have tried to do is to make each section free-standing and useful in itself, while allowing readers to cross-reference as appropriate.

We are very grateful for the advice and support which many readers of the pilot edition of this book supplied. In particular, we received very useful feedback from many lecturers at De Montfort University and Liverpool John Moores University where we trialled sections from the book during staff development workshops. Particular thanks go to Liz McDowell of the University of Northumbria at Newcastle for many important comments, to Malcolm Plant of Nottingham Trent University for contributions on action research, and to John Richardson of the Assessment Issues Group of the Open Learning Foundation for spotting some gaps in our coverage, and to our colleagues in the group for stimulating ideas, encouragement and support. Thanks also to Trisha Little, University of Nottingham, for help with the manuscript. We will continue to welcome further feedback on this book. Please write to any of us, care of our publishers, and we will acknowledge your contributions in future editions.

Sally Brown, Phil Race and Brenda Smith
January 1996

Chapter 1 Developing Strategies And Structures For Assessment

In this chapter we give some suggestions about ways to formulate policies for assessment. Such policies are becoming essential. Firstly because students now expect to be able to know much more about how assessment works than was formerly the case and secondly all UK universities have been asked to produce a Learning and Teaching Strategy.

We have not attempted in this chapter to make suggestions about which aspects of assessment should be addressed by an assessment strategy – we feel that the whole book provides an agenda from which decisions about this should be drawn by individual institutions and course teams.

With many universities adopting modular approaches, it is no longer satisfactory to devolve assessment procedures and regulations to individual departments and schools. Students are quick to notice any discrepancies or differences in how assessment works for them from one module or course to another. Also, it is increasingly important to develop a unified approach to appeals procedures, and this is done more easily when a university has a clear, uniform policy. The number of cases where students have taken assessors or universities to court about assessment issues is growing!

Within the context of a university policy on assessment, much of the detail can be devolved to course teams. In particular, changes to be introduced, such as diversifying the range of assessment processes in use, are best implemented at course level.

We next turn our attention to values. We feel it is important that assessment policies and strategies should be underpinned by certain values or ethics. We hope that our suggestions will help colleagues to implement assessment procedures which are as fair as we can make them, and which do not, by their nature, disadvantage individuals or groups of students when the overall picture of their assessment is considered.

Finally in this chapter, we offer some comments about the timing of assessment. Traditionally, assessment was often left till the end of a period of study. There is now greater emphasis on coursework assessment throughout the period of study, and the timing of this can cause students problems unless it is well thought out.

1

University-wide strategies

It is often said that a top-down and bottom-up approach gets the best of both worlds. The process of developing an institution-wide strategy for assessment provides opportunities for at least some of the staff in an institution to consider deeply the issues involved in assessment.

1 **Why develop a strategy?** If the document will just sit on shelves, don't bother! What will happen afterwards needs to be addressed. A strategy can help ensure a coherent approach across an institution, and make it easier to provide equivalence of experience for students. A strategy can also cater for ways of sharing best practice.

2 **Who should write the strategy?** The more people from throughout the institution that can be involved, the more likely they are to feel a sense of ownership of the strategy. It is worth thinking carefully about representation. A mixture of policy makers and grassroots lecturers is usually the best combination.

3 **Consult widely on the draft strategy.** Even though it may delay the implementation of policy, it is worth the time and energy needed for effective consultation. This allows the strategy to be placed on the agendas of faculty and department boards. It makes sense to look at the policies of other institutions, and to build on their better elements.

4 **Involve the Students' Union.** Students quite rightly feel very strongly about assessment. Listen to them carefully and take their views seriously. A policy backed by students is far easier to implement.

5 **Think about dissemination of the strategy.** How best can staff and students be informed? Use all available means to communicate the main points, including staff and student newsletters, memos to course leaders, and electronic means of communication.

6 **Decide how to make the strategy work.** This is the hardest part! Decide whether one person should spearhead the implementation of the strategy, or whether faculties and departments should take local responsibility for implementing it. Set target dates to build up a staged implementation.

7 **Be patient.** Major changes don't happen overnight, as both staff and students have strong views about assessment. Expect some alterations to existing policy to take at least a year to implement.

8 **Consider whether a staff development event would help.** A series of staged workshops around the institution can be valuable for sharing ideas, strategies and anxieties. Think carefully about who should attend such workshops, and what the expected outcomes should be.

9 **Think about the resource implications.** Think about the costs of staff abatement, workshop materials, and documents. When senior management is really committed to a strategy, the resources needed are usually forthcoming.

10 **Evaluate and revise as appropriate.** Build in an evaluation strategy from the beginning, and don't be afraid to make modifications on the basis of experience.

2

Course team strategies

Probably the most effective way of introducing major improvements in assessment is when they are planned by course teams rather than controlled by individual lecturers. We present below some questions that may make useful starting points for course team discussions about assessment.

1 **Is assessment to be addressed as an integral part of the course design process?** Does the team review assessment on an annual basis? Are assessments integrated across the course, or are they produced by a group of tutors?

2 **Are relevant assessment criteria identified and used by all team members?** Discussing criteria in a team usually leads to clarification and simplification of the criteria, making them easier for students (and staff) to understand.

3 **Are the assessment methods transparent to everyone?** It is important that they are not only understood by staff and students, but also by employers and other people who may need to know exactly what is being measured and how it is being approached.

4 **Are assessment workloads realistic?** Has the team anticipated what the workloads will be and how they will be shared out? Are workloads such that students and staff can cope with them? It can be very useful to plot the workloads of typical students when considering the amounts of assessment.

5 **Are the assessment tasks practicable?** Can they be completed with the available resources? For example, do students have sufficient access to computers, learning materials, and other resources they may need? Work out what the financial implications of assessment tasks will be, and also whether the assessment programme can be completed within the time available.

6 **Are the assessments free of bias?** Check that tasks are equally appropriate for males and females. Check that the assessments do not discriminate between students of different culture or language. It is worth giving a person in the course team responsibility to keep a running check on these aspects. It may be worth considering policies, such as whether overseas students should be allowed to take dictionaries into exams.

7 **Does the course team employ an appropriate range of different assessment methods?** If essays are used as the only form of assessment, students' writing skills may improve, but their skills at giving presentations may remain undeveloped. Use a grid showing which assessment methods are used for which purposes.

8 **How does the course team monitor whether students receive sufficient feedback on their work?** How much time is devoted to providing feedback, compared to the time involved in setting and marking work, attending exam boards, and keeping assessment records?

9 **Are the important learning outcomes being assessed adequately?** Asking this question at course team level can help the team to tease out some aspects of learning that may be hard to assess, but where it is very important to try to assess them.

10 **How is the team planning to monitor the effectiveness and reliability of each kind of assessment?** For example, as assessment is such an important aspect of teaching and learning, it may be sensible to reserve some meetings of the course team specifically for discussion about assessment.

3

Values of assessment

When snowed under by the amount of assessment we have to do, it is only too easy to dive into the task without taking the time to think out our moral or ethical stance for the task. We've taken some time to do this now, and identified ten values as a starting point on this mission. Several later sections in this book give further detail on how these values can be met.

1 **Assessment should be valid.** It should assess what it is that you really want to measure. For example, when attempting to assess problem-solving skills, the assessment should not be dependent on the quality and style of the production of written reports on problem solving, but on the quality of the solutions devised.

2 **Assessment should be reliable.** If we can get the task briefings, assessment criteria and marking schemes right, there should be good inter-tutor reliability when more than one tutor marks the work, as well as good intra-tutor reliability (tutors should come up with the same results when marking the same work on different occasions). All assignments should be marked to the same standard.

3 **Assessment should be fair.** Students should have equal opportunity to succeed even if their experiences are not identical. This is particularly important when assessing work based on individual learning contracts. It is also important that all assessment instruments and processes should be seen to be fair by all students.

4 **Assessment should be equitable.** Assessment practices should not discriminate between students, and should disadvantage no individual or group. Obviously, students may prefer and do better at different kinds of assessment (some love exams and do well in them, while others are better at giving presentations for example). So, a balanced diet of different means of assessment within a course will ensure that no particular group is favoured over any other group.

5 **Assessment should be formative.** Assessment is a time-consuming process for all concerned, so it seems like a wasted opportunity if it is not used as a means of letting students know how they are doing, and how they can improve. Assessment that is primarily summative in its function (for example when only a number or grade is given) gives students very little information, other than frequently confirming their own prejudices about themselves.

6 **Assessment should be timely.** Assessment that occurs only at the end of a learning programme is not much use in providing feedback, and also leads to the 'sudden death' syndrome, where students have no chance to practise before they pass or fail. Even where there is only end-point formal assessment, earlier opportunities should be provided for rehearsal and feedback.

7 **Assessment should be incremental.** Ideally, feedback to students should be continuous (rather than continual, as students often feel it is!). There is sense, therefore, in enabling small units of assessment to build up into a final mark or grade. This avoids surprises, and can be much less stressful than systems in which the whole programme rests on performance during a single time-limited occasion.

8 **Assessment should be redeemable.** Most universities insist that all assessment systems contain within them opportunities for the redemption of failure when things go wrong. This is not only just, but avoids high drop-out or failure rates.

9 **Assessment should be demanding.** Assessment systems should not be a pushover, and the assurance of quality is impossible when students are not stretched by assessment methods. That is not to say that systems should only permit a fixed proportion of students to achieve each grade: a good assessment system should permit all students considered capable of undertaking a course of study to have a chance of succeeding in the assessment, provided they learn effectively and work hard.

10 **Assessment should be efficient.** Brilliant systems of assessment can be designed which are completely unmanageable because of ineffective use of staff time and resources. The burden on staff should not be excessive, nor should be the demands on students undertaking the assessment tasks.

4

Choosing the right time for assessment

We have all encountered those stressful periods in an academic year when students feel overburdened with assessment, and when we feel overstretched with marking. The following suggestions provide some alternatives to this.

1 **Spread the assessment out throughout the semester or year.** Bunching all assessments towards the end makes it very difficult for any formative kind of feedback to be given to students. This could mean that (for example) students giving poor conclusions to essays could end up being marked down for this on five or six occasions.

2 **Assess a little rather than a lot.** Choose carefully what you really want to measure, and design tasks which measure this primarily. Don't measure the same skills again and again. You can often get just as good a comparative picture of how a class is doing from short assignments as you can from long comprehensive ones (and short ones take less time to mark, allowing feedback to be given to students more rapidly).

3 **Ask students to decide on agreed hand-in dates.** This helps students to feel a sense of ownership of the spread of assessment.

4 **Remember that students have a social life too!** Giving a test on the last day before a vacation is not the most effective time to plan assessment, and is certainly not popular with students.

5 **Think creatively.** Some staff insist they can only assess their students at the end of a course or module. However, many assessed tasks can usefully be set early on, including literature searches, book reviews, reflective logs and action plans.

6 **Sometimes design assignments on things that students have not yet covered.** This can be a very effective way of alerting students to what they need to learn in due course. It helps students become more receptive when the topics concerned are addressed later in the teaching programme.

7 **Adhere to deadlines firmly.** For example, say that a given assignment can only be marked if handed in on time, or that no marks can be awarded to late submitters once their colleagues have had their work returned to them. Offer to provide feedback, but no marks, when work is handed in late. In practice, however, make exceptions for documented illness, genuine crises, and so on.

8 **Try to time your assignments to avoid the 'week 7 nightmare'.** Students often report the phenomenon of everyone giving them coursework at the same time, and this often falls around midway through a semester in modularised systems. In the best universities, assessment dates are preplanned and timed to avoid such clashes, and are published at the beginning of each module.

9 **Get ahead of your colleagues!** If there is no policy in your department on timing assessments, set your most important coursework task really early. This may mean retiming associated lectures and tutorials so that students are equipped to start your task. It helps if, when students are doing your major piece of coursework, they are not snowed under with everyone else's assignments.

10 **Choose hand-in deadlines at 1600h on Tuesdays!** This allows late running students a weekend to catch up in, and allows students who are weekending away a Monday to travel back on!

Chapter 2 Managing Your Assessment

Our aim in this chapter is to offer suggestions which will help colleagues to assess. We start by making some general recommendations to bear in mind when choosing which assessment methods to employ. Advice on how to go about using each of these methods is provided later in the book.

We provide next a checklist on possible reasons for assessing. We feel that this will give further help in ensuring that the most appropriate methods of assessment are chosen for different contexts and levels. We then look more closely at what is to be measured, and give suggestions which should help colleagues identify the assessment criteria which will be the basis of each and every method they select.

We then move to three aspects of assessment where growing numbers of students make the assessment methods used previously harder to manage. With large student numbers it is increasingly important that we maintain records of assessment in ways that are effective, efficient and manageable. We offer some recommendations about how to keep the magnitude of the task of assessing students' work within reasonable bounds. For the occasions when we nonetheless end up with large amounts of student work to assess in a limited time, we offer suggestions based on our own experience of coping with 'big piles'.

Assessment is an essential and inescapable part of the job of teaching in higher or further education. With larger numbers of students, it is possible for the task to become tedious, so we end this chapter by offering some suggestions for making our task less boring.

5

Choosing the most appropriate methods of assessment

The range of assessment methods to choose from is much wider than is often realised. Yet more than 80% of assessment in universities comprises essays, reports, and traditional time-constrained exams. Assessment that is 'fit for purpose' uses the best method of assessment appropriate to the context, the students, the level, the subject and the institution. To help you choose the most appropriate methods, here are some questions to stimulate your thinking.

1 **Which, if any, of the following written elements should you choose from?** Consider the best uses of essays, reports, reviews, summaries, dissertations, theses, annotated bibliographies, case studies, journal articles, presentations, and exams.

2 **Should the method be time constrained?** Exams, phase tests and in-class activities might well be the most appropriate for the occasion. Time constrained tests put students under pressure, but are usually fairly good at preventing cheating.

3 **Is it important that the method you choose includes cooperative activity?** If it is important, you might choose to assess students in groups, perhaps on group projects, poster displays, or presentations.

4 **Is a visual component important?** When it is important, you might choose portfolios, poster displays, 'critique' sessions or exhibitions.

5 **Is it important that students use information technology?** When it is important, computer-based assessments may be best, getting students to answer multiple-choice questions, write their own programmes, prepare databases, write information stacks for hypertext, or write material for use in CD-ROM systems or on the Internet.

6 **Do you wish to try to assess innovation or creativity?** Some assessment methods that allow students to demonstrate these talents include performances, exhibitions, poster displays, presentations, projects, student-led assessed seminars, simulations and games.

7 **Are you keen to encourage students to develop oral skills?** If so, you might choose to assess vivas, presentations, recorded elements of audio and video tapes made by students, discussions, seminars, interviews or simulations.

8 **Do you want to assess the ways in which students interact together?** You might then assess negotiations, debates, rôle plays, interviews, selection panels, and case studies.

9 **Is the assessment of learning undertaken away from the institution important?** For example you may wish to assess learning done in the work place, in professional contexts or on field courses. You may choose to assess logs, reflective journals, field studies, case studies or portfolios.

10 **Is your aim to establish what students are able to do already?** Then you could try diagnostic tests (paper-based or technology-based), profiles, records of achievement, portfolios, interviews, and vivas.

6

Why should we assess?

Thinking clearly about our reasons for assessment helps to clarify which particular methods are best suited for our purposes, as well as helping to identify who is best placed to carry out the assessment, and when and where to do it. Some of the most common reasons for assessing students are referred to below.

1 **To classify or grade students.** There are often good reasons for us to classify the level of achievements of students individually and comparatively within a cohort. Assessment methods to achieve this will normally be summative and involve working out numerical marks or letter grades for students' work of one kind or another.

2 **To enable student progression.** Students often cannot undertake a course of study unless they have a sound foundation of knowledge or skills. Assessment methods to enable student progression therefore need to give a clear idea of students' current levels of achievement, so that they (and we) can know if they are ready to progress.

3 **To guide improvement.** The feedback students receive helps them to improve. Assessment that is primarily formative need not necessarily count towards any final award and can therefore be ungraded in some instances. The more detailed the feedback we provide, the greater is the likelihood that students will have opportunities for further development.

4 **To facilitate students' choice of options.** If students have to select options within a programme, an understanding of how well (or otherwise) they are doing in foundation studies will enable them to have a firmer understanding of their current abilities in different subject areas. This can provide them with guidance on which options to select next.

5 **To diagnose faults and enable students to rectify mistakes.** Nothing is more demotivating than continually getting bad marks and not knowing what is going wrong. Effective assessment lets students know where their problems lie, and provides them with an essential tool to put things right.

6 **To give us feedback on how our teaching is going.** If there are generally significant gaps in student knowledge, this often indicates faults in the teaching in the areas concerned. Excellent achievement by a high proportion of students is often due to high quality facilitation of student learning.

7 **To motivate students.** As students find themselves under increasing pressure, they tend to become more and more strategic in their approaches to learning, only putting their energies into work that counts. Assessment methods can be designed to maximise student motivation, and prompt their efforts towards important achievements.

8 **To provide statistics for the course, or for the institution.** Universities need to provide funding agencies with data about student performance, and assessment systems need to take account of the need for appropriate statistical information.

9 **To enable grading and final degree classification.** Unlike some overseas universities, UK universities still maintain the degree classification system. However, some universities are already debating the introduction of a no-classifications system coupled with the production of student portfolios.

10 **To add variety to students' learning experience, and add direction to our teaching.** Utilising a range of different assessment methods spurs students to develop different skills and processes. This can provide more effective and enjoyable teaching and learning.

7

Working out what you really want to assess

Very often, we find that we are assessing not what we really want to assess, but what happens to be easy to assess. 'If you can assess it, it probably isn't it' is one way of summarising the dilemma. It's important, therefore, to be very clear about what we are actually committed to assess. To set you thinking, you can ask yourself the following questions about each assessment task you use. (The way we've written these questions may suggest certain polarities to you, but your answers may well lie halfway along the spectrum in many cases!)

1 **Is it product or process that is to be assessed?** Are we concentrating in this particular assessment task on the actual outcome (maybe a report, essay, or artefact) or are we looking at how the students achieved the outcome?

2 **Is it specific subject knowledge that we test, or is it how well students can use such information?** Does the method of assessment prioritise the need for information recall and regurgitation, or is the knowledge involved needed as a background for synthesis, analysis and evaluation by students?

3 **Is it individual effort or team effort that is to be assessed?** Teamwork is valued by employers, tutors and the students themselves, and sometimes it is most appropriate to assess students in groups. On other occasions, the performance of individuals needs to be most clearly differentiated.

4 **Is it teaching or learning that is being assessed?** Are the assessment tasks student-centred? Are the tasks designed to allow students to demonstrate to what extent their learning has succeeded?

5   **Is assessment primarily formative or summative?** Are marks or grades needed by students at this point, or is this assessment task primarily there to allow students to receive feedback? There is little point writing detailed comments on final year degree scripts if students will never be able to read them!

6   **Is the assessment convergent or divergent?** Are all students aiming to achieve identical results ('right answers'), or are the assessment tasks designed to enable students to demonstrate individuality and diversity? Both approaches may well be appropriate within a given course at different stages.

7   **Is the methodology continuous or end-point?** If it is continuous, there may be opportunities for redemption of failure without the risk on any particular element of assessment being too high. If assessment methodology is end-point, then students will need to be made aware of this and prepared for it.

8   **Does the assessment encourage deep, surface, or strategic learning?** Encouraging deep learning has implications for course design. When students are over-assessed, most will learn at a surface or strategic level only.

9   **Is the assessment holistic or serialist?** Does the assignment give students an opportunity to integrate material from a variety of sources, or is it a discrete element, relating to a specific aspect of learning? Which approach is the most appropriate for the context in which you are working?

10   **Is the assessment time/context specific, or is it ipsative?** Does it measure achievement at a fixed point in time, or the extent of individuals' development from their earlier starting points?

11   **Is the assessment norm-referenced or criterion-referenced?** Does it measure a student's achievement in relation to that of other students, or does it enable students' achievements to be measured against a set of criteria? In the first instance, there is a tendency to have fixed pass/fail rates, whereas with criterion referencing, everyone who achieves the criteria will have passed.

8

Keeping good records of assessment

Though assessment is one of the most important tasks we do, it is important that we do not forget to keep good records of this aspect of our work. This takes time, but can save time and problems in the long run. The following suggestions may help you organise your record-keeping.

1 **Be meticulous.** However tired you are at the end of a marking session, record all the marks immediately (or indeed continuously as you go along). Then put the marks in a different place to the scripts. Then, should any disasters befall you (briefcase stolen, house burned down and so on), there is the chance that you will still have the marks even if you don't have the scripts any longer (or vice versa).

2 **Be systematic.** Use class lists, when available, as the basis of your records. Otherwise make your own class lists as you go along. File all records of assessment in places where you can find them again. It is possible (all three authors agree!) to spend as much time looking for missing marksheets as it took to do the original assessment!

3 **Use technology to produce assessment records.** Keep marks on a grid on a computer, and save the grid by date as a new file every time you add to it, so you are always confident that you are working with the most recent version. If you are as neurotic as your authors, you will also wish to keep paper copies of each list as an insurance against disaster!

4 **Use technology to save you from number-crunching.** The use of computer spreadsheet programs can allow the machine to do all of the sub-totalling, averaging and data handling for you. If you are afraid to set up a system for yourself, a computer-loving colleague or a member of information systems support staff will be delighted to start you off.

5 **Keep backup copies of all assessment data.** This applies whether the data are on paper or on disc. Simply photocopying a handwritten list of marks is a valuable precaution. Remind yourself how serious it would be if some of your records of assessment were irretrievably lost. Keep copies at work, at home, and in a deposit box at your bank if you're really paranoid!

6 **Keep files, not piles.** For example, keep a file for each student, or for each seminar group, as well as a file showing all the data for one assignment from the whole class.

7 **Post on-going assessment grids on your door or on a student notice board.** This not only helps you keep up your records, but spurs on students who are late submitting work when they see gaps alongside their names.

8 **Use other people.** Some universities employ administrative staff to issue and collect work for assessment, and to make up assessment lists and input the data into computers. Partners, friends and even young children can help you check your addition of marks, and help you record the data.

9 **Involve students.** Give students a full print-out of the mark sheet after each piece of work has been returned to a class, and let them check their own scripts against the master copy. When working with large groups, it is only too easy to transpose marks accidentally. Students will let you know very quickly if the mark on your records is less than the mark you wrote on their scripts!

10 **Assemble evidence of your organisational skills.** Being well organised in your assessment record-keeping not only saves you from headaches; it also contributes to the evidence you can use to demonstrate an important dimension of your professionalism as a teacher.

9

Reducing the burden of assessment

More and more university teachers are finding that the burden of assessment is becoming unmanageable. We know that formative assessment is one of the best ways of promoting student learning, but as student numbers rise and class sizes grow larger, we have to look at ways of coping with the greater workloads of assessment, without short-changing students. We offer a number of strategies below.

1 **Reduce the number of assignments.** Especially following changes in course design (modularisation or unitisation, for example), we often find ourselves assessing large numbers of assignments. We can ask ourselves if all of these are strictly necessary, and whether it is possible to combine some of them, and completely delete others.

2 **Reduce the word length on assignments.** Often we ask for 2,000, 3,000 or 5,000 word assignments, when half the length could be just as acceptable if the content were appropriate. This does not mean that students should be advised to 'stop when you have written x words' but instead they should be told to condense their first long drafts or sometimes to provide summaries instead of full assignments.

3 **Use assignment return sheets.** These can be forms which contain the assessment criteria for an assignment, with spaces for ticks/crosses, grades, marks and brief comments. They enable rapid feedback on 'routine' assessment matters, providing more time for individual comment to students, when necessary, on deeper aspects of their work.

4 **Consider using statement banks.** These are a means whereby frequently repeated comments can be listed on a sheet of paper to be stapled to student work, or put onto overhead transparencies for discussion in a subsequent lecture. (For more detail on these see Brown, Rust and Gibbs, 1994.)

5 **Think about different kinds of assignment.** Perhaps some essays or long reports could be replaced by shorter reviews, articles, memorandum reports or summaries. Projects could be assessed by poster displays instead of reports, and exam papers could include some sections of multiple-choice questions particularly where these could be marked by optical mark scanners.

6 **Involve students in peer-assessment.** Start small, and explain what you are doing and why. Peer-assessment can provide students with very positive learning experiences. At the start, it can be less threatening for students to assess work from a previous group (with names deleted).

7 **Encourage student self-assessment.** This is a very valuable skill in its own right for students to acquire. It is important to give students some feedback on how well they have done self-assessment. It is quicker to monitor student self-assessment than to do all the assessment yourself.

8 **Mark some exercises in class time using self- or peer-marking.** This is sometimes useful when students have prepared work expecting tutor-assessment, and have therefore prepared it to the standard that they wish to be seen by you. Assessing work in class gives time and opportunity for valuable debates about criteria and standards.

9 **Don't count all assessments.** For example, give students the option that their best five out of eight assignments will count as their coursework mark. Students satisfied with their first five need not undertake the other three at all then.

10 **Don't measure the same thing time and time again.** Collaborate with colleagues on other courses, and look for overlaps between assignments, and agree where these can be cancelled out.

10

Coping with big piles

No one wants to have to cope with huge piles of coursework scripts or exam papers, and we've already suggested some ways of avoiding this. However, not all factors may be within your control, and you may still end up with big piles! The following solutions, gained through painful experience by your authors, may be somewhat soothing at such times!

1 **Put the great unmarked pile under your desk.** It is very discouraging to be continually reminded of the magnitude of the overall task. Put only a handful of scripts or assignments in sight – about as many as you might expect to deal with in about an hour.

2 **Remember how to eat an elephant!** The only way is one bite at a time. Don't overload yourself; break up the big task into lots of manageable elements.

3 **Build yourself a reward strategy.** Follow your own vices or virtues! We know a lot about comfort eating. Comfort drinking, however, is counter-productive!

4 **Set yourself progressive targets.** Plan to accomplish a bit more at each stage than you need to. Build in safety margins. This allows you some insurance against unforeseen disasters (and kids), and can allow you, gradually, to earn some time off as a bonus.

5 **Make an even better marking scheme.** Often, it only becomes possible to make a really good marking scheme after you've found out the ways that candidates are actually answering the questions.

6 **Put the marking scheme where you can see it easily.** It can be useful to stick it up above your desk or table, so you don't have to rummage through your papers very time you need it to help you make a decision about how many marks have been earned.

7 **Mark in different places!** Mark at work, at home, and anywhere else that's not public. This means, of course, carrying scripts around as well as your marking scheme (or a copy of it). It does, however, avoid one place becoming so associated with doom and depression that you develop place-avoidance strategies for it!

8 **Mark one question at a time through all the scripts, at first.** This allows you to become quickly skilled at marking that question, without the agenda of all the rest of the questions on your mind. It also helps ensure reliability and objectivity of marking.

9 **When you've completely mastered your marking scheme for all questions, start marking whole scripts.** Now that you don't often need refer to the marking scheme, you will find that marking different questions provides a change (not quite as good as a rest, however!).

10 **Build up a re-marking agenda.** Every now and then, you'll make a decision about marking which you will need to implement retrospectively. It can be really time consuming to go back straightaway looking through all the scripts you have marked to see if changes to your marking are needed. It is more efficient to wait till you've got two or three things to check up regarding adjustments to the marked pile.

11

Making assessment less boring

Students and staff can all find assessment very boring. The following set of suggestions may serve as a menu from which you can choose, to add variety and even fun to your assessment. Select those choices that you feel are appropriate to your working context and method of teaching.

1 **Build in diversity.** All methods of assessment disadvantage some students, whether they are slow writers, poor orally, less able graphically, technophobic or whatever. Try to build up a range of methods of assessment to ensure that the same students aren't disadvantaged all the time. This also provides both you and them with variety.

2 **Involve students.** When assessment is a private matter between a tutor who knows a lot and students who are trying to maximise the amount they know, it can be boring. Using self- and peer-assessment can encourage a greater degree of commitment and involvement.

3 **Involve other colleagues.** When several tutors are assessing together it lightens the load (so long as they are all working along the same lines). Bringing in colleagues from other disciplines on assignments can be broadening, and can make for a more collegial approach to assessment.

4 **Bring in outsiders.** Employers can be a useful addition to the assessment team, when you can find means to motivate them to be involved. In professional areas, it can be useful to involve clients as assessors: who better, for example, can assess whether patients are being lifted effectively in nursing courses than the patients themselves?

5 **Vary the location.** Poster assessment, for example, can take place in public areas of the university such as foyers and exhibition areas rather than the classroom. This allows students to celebrate achievement, and can be popular also with senior staff, quality assessors and so on.

6 **Have a quickie sometimes!** Very short, in-class assessments marked on the spot, and counting for a small proportion of marks, can form part of an assessment programme. Such assessments can be popular with students as they provide instant feedback and on-the-spot responses to issues and questions.

7 **Consider using technology.** Computer-based assessment can be used from time to time even on non-technological courses, and can make a change from time-constrained written assignments. Computer-based assessments can give the bonus of helping arts and social science students to become more literate regarding information technology.

8 **Give students chances to assess you in informal sessions.** They can learn a lot by being given the chance to frame questions, devise mark schemes, and test you out. It also helps students to see you as one of the resources they can use and learn from, rather than the fount of all knowledge! (It can feel a bit risky, and take a bit of confidence on your part, however!)

9 **Extract 'howlers' and share them kindly!** This can be a fun way of alerting learners to some of the things that can go awry in essays and exam answers (but be careful to preserve anonymity unless you know that the originator can see the funny side too).

10 **Add a couple of marks for 'fun'!** For example, in formative assessments such as essays or reports, invite students to provide an additional 20-word fun postscript, for example a non-serious definition of a jargon term.

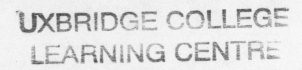

Chapter 3 Learning Through Assessment

Although this chapter is short, we believe that it is probably one of the most important topics in the book. It is essential to remember how large a role assessment can play in learning. In particular, the feedback we give students on their performance can be a vital incentive to them, and can help them take greater control of their own learning. Throughout this book, in fact, we return to the importance of giving students feedback, and facilitating ways of them receiving feedback from each other, and, indeed, assessing their own learning.

We offer next some suggestions on ways to employ assessment to help students to develop their approaches to studying. One of the most significant outcomes of a period in higher or further education is learning how to learn, and how to manage the processes involved. This is so crucial that we believe it should not be left to chance, or survival of the fittest. We need to provide students with opportunities to develop appropriate fitness, and one of the best ways of ensuring that they take such development seriously is for us to confirm that we take it seriously by including work relating to study-skills development in our assessment menu.

However much students have learned, their assessment still depends on the effectiveness of the ways that they demonstrate their learning when they are assessed. Each and every method of assessment requires its own set of skills and competences, over and above the subject knowledge or skills being assessed. We end this chapter with some suggestions about how we can help students identify and address the skills which they need, to prove that their learning has been successful.

12

Giving feedback on assessed work

If, as we believe, assessment is the 'engine that drives learning', then the way in which we give feedback is an important way of gearing the engine so that maximum effect is achieved from the effort put in by all concerned. We suggest the following mixture of criteria for feedback, and suggestions for ensuring that students get as much feedback as is possible. As you will see, we've come up with rather more than ten suggestions for this important area!

1 **Feedback should be targeted to enhance learning.** Feedback should concentrate on what to do to improve. This is better than when feedback is heavily judgemental.

2 **Feedback should be timely.** When marked work is returned to students months after submission, feedback is often totally ignored because it bears little relevance to students' current needs. Many universities nowadays specify in their Charters or Partnership Agreements that work should be returned within two to three weeks, enabling students to derive greater benefits from feedback.

3 **Think about how students will feel when they get marked work back.** Students can be in states of heightened emotion at such points. If their scripts are covered with comments in red ink (even when it is all praise) it is rather intimidating for them at first.

4 **Try to do more than put ticks.** Tempting as it is to put ticks beside things that are correct or good, ticks don't give much real feedback. It takes a little longer to add short phrases such as 'good point', 'I agree with this', 'yes, this is it', 'spot on', and so on, but such comments do much more to motivate students than just ticks.

5 **Avoid putting crosses if possible.** Students often have negative feelings about crosses on their work, often carried forward from schooldays. Short phrases such as 'no', 'not quite', 'but this wouldn't work' and so on, can be much better ways of alerting students to things that are wrong.

6 **Try to make your writing legible.** (We try, and fail, here!) If there is not going to be room to make a detailed comment directly on the script, put code numbers or asterisks, and write your feedback on a separate sheet. A useful compromise is to put feedback comments on post-its stuck to appropriate parts of a script, but it's worth still using a code, asterisk or some such device so that if students remove the post-its as they read through their work, they can still work out exactly which points your comments apply to.

7 **Feedback can be very quick.** For example, self-assessment exercises can be set for which you have already written the feedback comments applying to the choices made in multiple-choice or structured questions. When feedback is received very quickly, it is much more effective, as students can still remember exactly what they were thinking as they addressed each question.

8 **Feedback can be instantaneous!** Computer-marked assessment formats can be used purely to deliver rapid feedback. Multiple-choice questions on screen can allow students to make decisions at their own pace (privately, or with fellow-students), and get instant feedback (devised by you) on whether their choices were the best ones. More importantly, you can use such means to give them instant feedback on why other choices were less good or entirely wrong.

9 **Feedback can be given before work is assessed.** For example, as soon as a class hands in a piece of work, you can issue handouts of model answers and discussions of the main things that may have caused problems. Students can read such information while their own efforts are still fresh in their minds, and can derive a great deal of feedback straight away. You can then concentrate, while assessing, on giving them *additional* feedback individually, without going into detail on things that you have already addressed in the general discussion comments you have already given them.

10 **Feedback should be positive.** It is sometimes difficult to find something good to say about a piece of work! Ideally, however, you should start by commenting on a positive aspect before leading into a criticism.

11 **Feedback should be detailed.** It can be difficult to achieve this when time is limited, but the more indication you can give students about what is right and wrong, the more opportunities they have to learn from your feedback.

12 **Feedback should be efficient.** Work undertaken by the Oxford Centre for Staff Development 'Teaching More Students' project team indicated that the time taken over assessment on many courses was much greater than the time devoted to teaching and learning. Assessment systems should be devised to maximise the amount of feedback given to students within the time available. Such methods include the use of assignment return sheets, statement banks, and computer marked assignments.

13 **Feedback should be participative.** Feedback can be given to students in groups. This helps students become aware that they are not alone in making mistakes, and allows them to learn from the successes and failures of others. When giving one-to-one feedback, it is often useful to allow students the opportunity to interrogate you and challenge your comments (orally or in writing) so that any issues which are unclear can be resolved.

14 **Feedback should be realistic.** When making suggestions for improvement of student work, consider carefully whether they can be achieved. It may not have been possible (for example) for students to gain access to certain resources or books in the time available.

15 **Feedback should be fair.** Check that your feedback is not influenced by the amount of money that was spent on the work you mark (for example, some students can submit work produced by expensive desktop publishing systems, while other students have no access to such facilities).

16 **Feedback should be motivating.** Think carefully about the language you use, so that students are encouraged into doing (even) better next time. The use of 'final' language such as 'excellent' may be rewarding to hear or read, but offers no indication to the best students regarding how they may stretch themselves even further.

17 **Feedback should be honest.** When there are serious problems which students need to be made aware of, feedback comments should not avoid them. It may be best to arrange for individual face-to-face feedback sessions with some students, so you can monitor how they are taking any bad news and provide appropriate comfort at the same time.

18 **Feedback can be given before scores or grades.** Consider whether sometimes it may be worth returning students' work to them with feedback comments but no grades (but having written down your marks in your own records). Then invite students to try to work out what their scores or grade should be, and to report to you in a week's time what they think. This causes students to read all your feedback comments earnestly in their bid to work out how they have done. Most students will make good guesses regarding their grades, and it's also worth finding out which students are way out.

19 **Think whether audiotapes may be the best way of giving feedback.** In some subjects, it is quite hard to write explanatory comments on students' work. For example, in mathematics, it can be quicker and easier to 'talk' individual students through how a problem should be solved, referring to asterisks or code-numbers marked on their work. Such feedback has the advantage of tone of voice for emphasis and explanation. Another advantage is that students replay it until they have fully understood all of your feedback.

20 **Consider giving feedback by e-mail.** In some disciplines, students feel very relaxed when working at a computer terminal on their own. With e-mail, students can receive your feedback when they are ready to think about it. They can read it again later, and even file it. Using e-mail, you can give students feedback as you work through their scripts, rather than having to wait till you return the whole set to a class.

21 **Think about making a video.** For example, if you have marked a large cluster of essays or reports from a class, and there are a lot of issues you wish students to think about, it could be worth making a short video addressing the main problems students encountered. Students then have the advantages of facial expression as well as tone of voice, and can view the tape more than once if necessary. You could show the tape in a lecture and watch their reactions. The same video may be just as relevant on a future occasion when you may use the same assignment.

13

Using assessment to promote study-skills development

It is becoming more common for universities to provide modules on study-skills development, particularly for 1st-year or foundation-year students. These modules or courses work best when they are seen to be equal in status to normal subject-based courses. It is therefore necessary to have assessed tasks on these courses. The following suggestions may help you use such tasks to assist learners in developing their study-skills.

1 **Get students to do a 'SWOT' analysis of their learning styles.** Give out a grid with four boxes for strengths, weaknesses, opportunities and threats. Ask students to complete the grid, and to write a short reflective account on what they learned about themselves as a result of doing the task. Ask students to give themselves a score out of 20 for the depth of thinking they reckon that the task caused them to do.

2 **Get students to make a question bank.** This should be a set of (say) 300 short, sharp questions on the other topics they are currently studying. Suggest that they make a matching answer bank. Formats can include record cards, pocket notebooks or computer programs. Tutor-assess (or peer-assess) the product with (say) 10 marks for having 300 questions, 10 marks for 300 answers, 10 for the quality of the questions and answers, and 10 for students' creativity in designing the format of their question-banks.

3 **Get students in groups to compile a bibliography of study-skills resources in the library.** Encourage them to use on-line computer catalogues, computer searches and visual shelf-combing. Ask the group to produce a self-assessed mark for the comprehensiveness of the search and the accuracy of the referencing, and individual marks for the respective contributions of individuals to the final product.

4 **Get students to do an assessed review of a study-skills resource.** A limit of (say) 500 words is useful. Ask students to choose which resource to review from their research into what is available. Assess on content, style, and their personal evaluation of the resource.

5 **Get students to make a contribution to a computer conference.** This could be a book review, or an evaluation of a component of their course. Assess on content, style and originality, using either tutor-assessment or peer-assessment (blind) or a combination of both.

6 **Get students to produce a personal action plan for their studies of a subject.** Peer-assess on feasibility, interest and practicality.

7 **Get students to write a reflective log on their learning over a fortnight.** Ask them to record their feelings about effective (and futile!) learning experiences, and what they found out about themselves in each case. Self-assess on depth of thinking and usefulness of the process.

8 **Get students to make a revision timetable.** For example, ask them to plan for the last month before forthcoming exams. Assess (self or peer) on practicality, workability and interest.

9 **Get students to form learning syndicates.** Peer-assess the minutes and working notes of three meetings of each syndicate, using assessment criteria proposed by each syndicate.

10 **Get students to collaborate on producing essays on 'practical approaches to successful study'.** Peer-assess on criteria agreed by the whole class.

14

Preparing students to succeed in assessment

This is of course central to the purposes of teaching and learning, yet sometimes it can appear to students that assessment is there to catch them out rather than to allow them to demonstrate their achievements. The following suggestions may help you to bridge the gap between learning and assessment.

1 **Help students to understand assessment.** Help them to think about why assessment is needed, what is being measured, and how the measurements are being approached.

2 **Make assessment criteria clear.** Take the mystery away. Reveal the hidden agendas. Help students to know exactly what they should become able to do to succeed, however hard or complex it may seem at first.

3 **Give students confidence.** The more we can help students to see how assessment works, the more confident they are that they can prepare themselves to give their best.

4 **Help students to realise that assessors are human!** Share openly what it feels like to mark big piles of essays, reports or exam scripts, and how difficult it is to make sound assessment decisions unless the criteria are really explicit. Let them know that there is no magic involved!

5 **Give students safe opportunities for practice.** Provide chances for students to rehearse the skills which they will need to fare well in forthcoming assessments. Do this for each kind of assessment they will meet.

6 **Give students feedback on their techniques.** Don't just provide feedback on students' knowledge and understanding; give additional feedback on how well (or otherwise) they communicate their knowledge in writing or orally.

7 **Encourage students to help each other prepare for assessment.** Advise against private, lonely, competitive swotting! Suggest to students how much better they can learn by testing each other, explaining things to each other, and giving each other feedback. Student self-help groups can be enormously successful.

8 **Help students to manage their time.** Avoid the tendency to try to get students to learn yet more new things when it may be more important for them to concentrate on consolidating their existing knowledge in preparation for assessment.

9 **Explain different forms of assessment.** Help students to see why different processes are used, and what each type of assessment is intended to measure.

10 **Be ready to talk openly about assessment.** Help students to feel that you are 'on their side' rather than conspiring against them when it comes to assessment. This does not mean giving them clues regarding what they will be asked to do, or accidentally revealing the exam questions! As far as you can, open up the whole agenda of assessment to students, and give them direct advice about how best they can prepare to demonstrate that they have learned successfully.

Chapter 4 Assessment Quality Control

Assessing our students' work is the most important thing we ever do for them. Our assessments influence their whole lives and careers, so it is crucial that the quality of our assessment is as good as we can make it. Most universities have systems whereby the quality of courses is monitored and adjusted, and these particularly need to address the quality of assessment.

We believe that quality control starts best with lecturers themselves. We start this chapter with some suggestions for monitoring your own assessment. Doing this well can help to optimise fairness to students, and can also help you to avoid the difficult situations which can arise when there are grounds for students to appeal against assessment decisions. It is important for lecturers to see how their assessment 'spreads' students. The nature of such a spread will depend on whether norm-referencing is taking place (where a normal distribution curve of results may be expected with a large sample of students), or whether criterion-referencing is taking place (where a successful cohort of students could show a spread nothing like a normal distribution).

A vital role in ensuring the quality of assessment is played by external examiners. There is cause for concern, however, as to whether external examiners are allowed to take part sufficiently in all the related processes, and some evidence that there is sometimes an 'old colleagues network' in play. We start by offering some suggestions regarding how relationships with external examiners can be developed at a distance, preparing for opportunities to make the most of their expertise and perspective. We then offer some practical recommendations about ensuring that external examiners' visits go off smoothly – an essential prerequisite to allowing them to play a useful part on the day. External examiners themselves have a very significant contribution to make in improving the quality and diversity of assessment, and we continue with some suggestions specifically for them. External examiners' reports are important documents in the course monitoring and review processes, and we hope that our suggestions for writing these will help them have impact and direction.

With growing student numbers, there is increasing concern about plagiarism and cheating, particularly in the context of assessed coursework. While recommending, as we do, that the part played in the assessment profile of students by unseen written exams should be reduced, it is therefore important to take care that the incidence of plagiarism or cheating does not increase as a result. We offer some suggestions about avoiding this, not least regarding clarifying and legitimising the very real roles that collaborative work can take.

15

Monitoring the quality of your own assessment processes

However good we are at assessing students, we do well to monitor our effectiveness, and keep a watching brief on what works well and what does not, so that we too can learn from our triumphs and mistakes, and address problems. Quality assessors, both internal and external, also usually look for evidence of how quality is monitored.

1 **Keep an overview of the marks you are giving.** In a small sample it won't be possible to get a set of results which plot a normal distribution curve on a graph. However, if you notice that all of your marks are bunching too tightly at the median point, or that everyone is getting top marks, this may indicate that something is awry. It may help you to use a spreadsheet or other visual means to keep an eye on what's going on.

2 **Get students to give you feedback on how well they feel you are assessing them.** You may not always want to hear their answers, but you could ask questions including 'Am I giving you enough feedback?', 'Do you find it helps you to improve?', 'Is the turn around fast enough for you?', 'Is there any way in which I can improve my assessment?', 'How useful are the questions I am setting?', and so on.

3 **Get help from colleagues.** Especially when work is not double-marked, sampled or moderated, it is useful to get colleagues to take a look at some of your grades, particularly when you are inexperienced regarding assessment. Pick scripts, including a strong one, a weak one and an average one, and ask an experienced colleague or two to confirm that they agree with your evaluation.

4   **Keep notes from year to year.** As you assess sets of work, note any difficulties you experience which may have arisen from the timing of the assessment or how you briefed the students. Note also difficulties of interpretation. Use these notes to help you design better assessments in future years.

5   **Remember how valuable data on student performance is in its own right.** Use such data to identify areas where students generally showed strengths and weaknesses. Think ahead regarding ways in which future assessments may be adjusted to help students to address areas of weakness next time round.

6   **Beware of upward-creeping standards.** The more experienced you become in teaching and assessing a subject, the greater the risk is that you gradually expect or demand higher levels of performance from successive groups of students.

7   **Tune in to other universities.** Build up your list of friends and colleagues in other colleges, and exchange with them past exam papers, assignment briefings and marking schemes. This can help you design new tasks more easily for your own students, and also gives you the chance to seek feedback from such people on your own assessment practices.

8   **Stand back and ask 'what did that really measure?'** When reflecting on data from assignment performances or exam results, check that you did in fact succeed in measuring those aspects of student performance that you intended to assess. Also, ask 'what *else* did I measure?' Decide whether to make such additional agendas more explicit when they are valuable (or, when not valuable, how to steer assessment tasks away from such agendas).

9   **Use external reviewers.** Quality auditors or reviews may well provide you with comments on how effectively they perceive your assessment methods to be. Use such feedback to help you to improve continuously, rather than seeing it as a personal attack. Make sure that you continue to include those elements that they praise or commend, and develop such elements further when appropriate.

10   **Become an external reviewer yourself.** Once you have developed expertise in your own university, an excellent way to learn from the experiences of other institutions is to become involved in external examining or quality assessment yourself. What you learn about the excellence (or otherwise) of others' means of assessment can then be transferred to your own context.

16

Making good use of your external examiner at a distance

By definition, external examiners tend to be people not exactly on your doorstep. Therefore, quite a lot of your dealings with such people are likely to be by letter, fax, e-mail or telephone. Even so, care needs to be taken that your external examiners are tuned to the correct wavelength regarding your course and your institution.The following suggestions may help you to avoid problems with them.

1 **Send examiners welcome letters of introduction.** Explain to them how pleased you are that they have accepted the invitation to become external examiners, and how you look forward to working with them.

2 **Introduce your team.** A 'photo gallery' with brief details of areas of responsibility for each member of your team can help external examiners to tune in to your course even before their first visit. The same information may well be useful for the course handbook.

3 **Post them the university calendar.** Make sure they are informed of key dates, such as those of exam boards, well in advance. Let them know when they may expect work to moderate, questions to review, and the dates by which you will need to have things back from them. External examiners tend to be busy people, so make sure that they have leeway to negotiate alternative dates with you. Send them a university pack of information. This should include general regulations regarding assessment, as well as particular information showing how assessment works in your course.

4 **Clarify arrangements for fees and expenses.** Make sure that the normal low recompense for their efforts does not come as an unpleasant surprise to them.

5 **Help them to see the background and context of your course.** Tell them about the history of the course, and changes that have already been made to its structure and the way that it is assessed. Show them how the course relates to other programmes which may feed into it, and to follow-on programmes. Give them details of future plans regarding the development of the course.

6 **Involve your external examiners in developments.** Send them Minutes of Course Board meetings, particularly when assessment issues are featured. Don't present them with a fait accompli when changes are made – they may well have views which could usefully be addressed.

7 **Be truthful!** External examiners are experienced people, and trying to pull the wool over their eyes is not the best way to cement good working relationships with them!

8 **Encourage them to visit the course team early on.** Help them to get involved in the planning and evaluation of the course. Plan their visits carefully. Ask them what they would like to do and to see. Involve the course team as much as possible.

9 **Be clear regarding areas of responsibility.** External examiners have different kinds of experience, and may work in different ways for different courses and institutions. They need to know exactly how their role fits in to the way your course is examined and moderated.

10 **Invite external examiners to a training day.** Pay them appropriately for their time and participation. Some universities run half-day or full-day training programmes for external examiners to brief them collectively, and to give them the chance to see round the campus and facilities. Such programmes can be combined with visits to your course team and department.

17

Using your external examiner on the day

The days when your external examiner visits you represent precious time. The following suggestions may help you ensure that external examiners' visits go smoothly and happily, and may allow you to make the most of the opportunities that such times offer.

1 **Confirm that your examiner is indeed coming!** You may well have planned the date well ahead, but to give you peace of mind it is always a good idea to confirm the visit about a week before the event. External examiners have been known to forget to enter dates in their diaries!

2 **Send clear travel instructions.** Find out how examiners intend to travel. Ensure that they know how to find their way from the motorway or rail station to the university. Send them good local maps showing buildings that are easy to identify. Provide travel directions in large print, making it easier to see directions if driving.

3 **Check in advance whether an overnight stay is needed.** Even when examiners have previously always travelled on the day of the meeting, they may not necessarily be starting out from their home destinations this time, and may be heading somewhere else the day after your meeting. Confirm accommodation arrangements in writing with the hotel, and send copies to examiners.

4 **Arrange for examiners to be met.** If train travel is involved, it can be much appreciated if you meet them at the station and take them the rest of the way. If not, make sure that as soon as they arrive at the university there is someone to meet them. They may have been travelling for some time, and a friendly face to meet them makes a lot of difference.

5 **Plan the day carefully.** Try to build in some spare time. Things may not always go according to your plans. Examiners can be delayed by late trains or traffic problems, and it is worth making sure that any preliminary meetings can still take place. Involve examiners in the planning of the day. They may have things they want to discuss, especially after seeing a selection of student work.

6 **Think carefully about breaks and refreshments.** We all function better with a few regular breaks, and the availability of light refreshments during the day is usually welcomed, especially on arrival if a long distance has been travelled.

7 **Arrange for examiners to meet some students.** It is useful to draw up a brief agenda, so both examiners and students have a shared idea of the purposes of such meetings. You may need to put students' minds at rest (in case they become anxious), especially if it is the first time they have met an examiner.

8 **Arrange for examiners to meet members of the course team.** Ask examiners whether the work they have seen already has areas for praise or concern, and whether they want to discuss particular aspects of the course with the people involved in teaching it.

9 **Try to avoid surprises.** Examiners don't like being put on the spot during meetings about, for example, their views on proposed developments to the course, or on how problems should be addressed. It is helpful to them if such issues are shared with them before their visit.

10 **Regard the day as an opportunity for expert consultancy.** External examiners are chosen for their breadth of experience and expertise. Don't let the situation intimidate you. Listen to their advice. Solicit their suggestions and respond creatively rather than negatively to any criticisms they offer. After all, the whole aim of the external examiner system is to maintain and improve quality.

18

Being an external examiner yourself

It is flattering to be approached to undertake external examining. It is a recognition of your standing in your field, and of the experience you bring to your work. However, it is not all glory (and not usually well paid!). The following suggestions may help you do a good job as an external examiner.

1 **Ask yourself why you are doing the job.** Is it to gain experience, to improve your own courses, to meet new people, to be able to put it on your CV? Clarifying your own reasons for being an examiner will help you benefit more fully from the experience.

2 **Think about your commitment.** Have you enough time? What will your duties involve in practice? How many days will you need to be away from your own job? Can you afford the time? Talk to other external examiners. Compare approaches to the role. Build up a picture of which actions are reasonable and appropriate.

3 **Put dates in your diary as soon as you get them!** At the beginning of a new academic year, enter into your diary all of the dates on which you will be required to attend meetings. If you don't yet know what these dates are likely to be, it's worth asking for them, or choosing some dates yourself to keep available for meetings.

4 **Check the university regulations.** Many institutions are in the process of changing their regulations, so don't assume that regulations will be the same as in your own university – or even that they will be the same as they were last year if you are continuing as an examiner. If you have not been sent a copy of the regulations, ask for one.

5 **Arrange for a day visit.** This is particularly desirable if you are starting as a new external examiner for a course. It is worth spending a day getting to know the course team and the institution, and will give you a much clearer picture of your role and responsibilities.

6 **Take the job seriously.** Both sides benefit when external examiners approach their work with appropriate professionalism. If you've been sent scripts to look at for comments on standards, return them promptly with your conclusions. Set aside time at an appropriate point to write your report.

7 **Keep in touch with the course.** Developing your relationship with the course team can give you a good feel for the course. Ask to be sent, for information, minutes of course team meetings. Find out who is your most appropriate point of contact, for example, whether it should be the course leader you communicate with, or the head of the department responsible for the course.

8 **Get to know the students.** This is often the most enjoyable part of being an external examiner. It is a chance for you to gain insight into issues that are important to students. Take care, however, to balance student perspectives and aspirations with the resources available to the course, and the context within which the course operates.

9 **Find good things to say about the course.** Work out which features of the course should be commended and encouraged. Avoid the feeling that your main job is to spot things that are wrong.

10 **Back up any critical comments with practical, positive suggestions.** When a course team faces problems, external examiners can be a really valuable source of advice. Make sure that you're sufficiently tuned in to the course to be able to offer suggestions when asked, or when help is needed.

19

Writing external examiner's reports

External examiners' reports are a very public side of assessment. The words you write when composing such reports may be analysed and probed into very deeply by course teams – and quality assessors! The following suggestions could help you make best use of the responsibility you bear when writing such reports, especially if you are taking on external examining for the first time.

1 **Check your briefing carefully.** Your role should be clearly defined in the assessment regulations for the course, within the university's regulations.

2 **Get hold of your predecessor's reports.** External examiners normally serve for between three and five years, so it should be possible to see how your predecessor handled the role. It is particularly valuable to look for recommendations made in previous reports. You can check whether they are now being implemented by the course team, and you can include appropriate acknowledgement of this in your own report.

3 **Look for the main headings to address.** They may or may not have appeared as headings in previous reports, but (for example) the first paragraph often addresses whether the standard of the course is comparable with similar courses in other institutions.

4 **Comment on trends.** It is best not to go into too much specific detail in your reports: you can always save elaborations for your verbal contributions to the exam board.

5 **Keep your report simple.** External examiners' reports are often scrutinised by people who know little about the specific subject (for example, a 'Quality and Standards Committee'), and such people need to be able to identify the main messages in your report.

6 **Keep your report short.** If it's too long, your main points may get lost amid other details. Don't feel that you have to prove you've done a good job of being an external examiner by writing a very detailed report. The most valuable reports are ones that are concise and strong, and that make any recommendations very clearly.

7 **Make gentle recommendations.** It is far more acceptable to say 'It may be worthwhile for the course team to consider …' rather than 'It is essential that the following changes be implemented at once'.

8 **Consider getting informal feedback on your draft report.** For example, it is useful to send a copy of your draft to the course leader, inviting comments about anything you've missed, and suggestions for rewording. Sometimes course leaders can help you to include in your report appropriately phrased comments which will in due course help the course team to make improvements to the operation of the course.

9 **Build continuity into your reports.** When you are following up previous reports you have written for the course, look carefully for evidence showing that your earlier recommendations have been acknowledged and followed through.

10 **Structure your report systematically.** Consider using a system of numbered points, or headings and sub-headings, so people discussing your report can refer to a particular item easily. This can also make your reports easier to read and assimilate.

20

Plagiarism, cheating and assessment

In a book about assessment, we must not forget that things can go wrong when students don't approach their tasks in the ways in which we intend them to do so. For assessment to work fairly, all parties must play the game. Plagiarism is usually interpreted as 'unfair or inappropriate usage of other people's work', while cheating is somewhat more sinister – though the borderlines between the two are impossible to define precisely. The following suggestions may help you to ensure that students know their responsibilities regarding fair play.

1 **Distinguish between malicious and inadvertent plagiarism.** Punitive action may be quite inappropriate when plagiarism is the consequence of students' lack of understanding of acceptable practice regarding citing the work of others.

2 **Debate issues and solutions with the whole class.** Establish ground rules for fair play, and agreed procedures for dealing with any infringements of these ground rules. It is important that such discussions should take place before the first assessment.

3 **Act decisively when you discover copying.** One option is to treat copying as collaborative work, and mark the work as normal but divide the total score by the number of students involved. Their reactions to this often help you find out who did the work first, or who played the biggest part in doing the work.

4 **Be alert when encouraging students to work together.** Make sure that they know where the intended collaboration should stop, and that you will be vigilant to check that later assessed work does not show signs of the collaboration having extended too far.

5 **Help students to understand the fine line between collaborative working and practices which the university will regard as cheating.** Sometimes it can come as a shock to students to find that what they thought of as acceptable collaboration is being regarded as cheating.

6 **Don't underestimate your students!** Clever students will always find a way to hack into computer marked assessments. Bear this in mind when considering whether to use such processes for assessment or just for feedback. (If students can hack into the security systems of NASA, your system may not be as safe as you may hope!)

7 **Anticipate problems, and steer round them.** When collaboration is likely to occur, consider whether you can in fact turn it into a virtue by redesigning the assessments concerned to comprise collaborative tasks for students in groups.

8 **Be aware of cultural differences regarding acceptable behaviour regarding tests.** Bring the possibility of such differences to the surface by starting discussions with groups of students. Acknowledge and discuss the extreme pressures to avoid failure to which some students may feel themselves subject.

9 **Get students to devise a code of practice.** Students actually want fair play, and can be very rigorous if asked to devise systems to guarantee this. Draw links between the systems they devise and the Assessment Regulations extant in your university. Make sure that students understand what the regulations mean!

10 **Remember how difficult it can be to prove that unfair practices have occurred.** Study the Appeals Procedures of your university. Remember that when things go wrong not all the blame will lodge firmly with any students who were guilty; when the blame hits the fan, it can land on you too!

Chapter 5 Methods Of Assessment

One of our principal aims in this book is to encourage colleagues to diversify assessment. We believe that by employing a wider range of assessment processes, it becomes more feasible to allow all students the opportunity of giving of their best in the ways that suit them best, and therefore avoiding discriminating against students who happen to be weak in one or two particular forms of assessment. This chapter contains practical suggestions for how to go about using a range of assessment formats which are alternatives to traditional examinations.

We start by looking at student presentations. When these are included as elements of assessment, they can provide students with valuable opportunities to practise and improve skills which will be sought by employers, and which will be useful throughout their professional careers.

We look next at dissertations and theses. One of the principal problems of assessing these is that they are necessarily individual pieces of work, and it is therefore hard to identify a common set of criteria with which to assess them.

Getting students to do reviews or annotated bibliographies is a very effective way of catalysing their attention on published work, and developing their critical skills. We offer suggestions about how to include such tasks as part of the assessment portfolio.

In many disciplines, it is important that students develop appropriate performance skills. Though these may be more complex to assess than subject knowledge, it is necessary that we are seen to be assessing them, or students may not take them sufficiently seriously.

We move next to ideas about ways of assessing poster displays and exhibitions. Producing these, and having them assessed, can be very productive for students in terms of the learning associated with the processes involved.

We move next to laboratory and practical work. In two sets of suggestions, we offer suggestions about how to set up such work in ways which allow it to contribute effectively and fairly to assessment.

We end this chapter by looking at ways in which students' contributions to seminar programmes may be assessed. We have identified some suggestions to add to those already made about the presentation aspects that can be associated with such programmes.

21

Assessing presentations

Being able to speak convincingly and authoritatively are useful career skills for students. One of the best ways of helping them develop such skills is to involve them in giving assessed presentations. The following suggestions may help your students get the most from such activities.

1   **Make the criteria for assessment of presentations clear from the outset.** Students will not then be working in a vacuum and will know what is expected of them.

2   **Get students involved in the assessment criteria.** This can be done either by allowing them to negotiate the criteria themselves or by giving them plenty of opportunities to question criteria you impose.

3   **Ensure that students understand the weighting of the criteria.** Help them to know whether the most important aspects of their presentations are to do with the *way* they deliver their contributions (voice, clarity of expression, articulation, body language, use of audio-visual aids, etc) or the *content* of their presentations (evidence of research, originality of ideas, effectiveness of argument, ability to answer questions, etc).

4   **Let the students have a mark-free rehearsal.** This gives students the chance to become more confident and to make some of the more basic mistakes at a point where it doesn't count against them. Constructive feedback is crucial at this point so that students can learn from the experience.

5   **Involve students in the assessment of their presentations.** When given the chance to assess each other's presentations they take them more seriously and will learn from the experience. Students merely watching each other's presentations tend to get bored and can behave badly. If they are evaluating each presentation using an agreed set of criteria, they tend to engage themselves more fully with the process, and in doing so learn more from the content of each presentation.

6 **Be realistic about what can be achieved.** It is not possible to get twelve 5-minute presentations into an hour, and presentations always tend to over-run. It is also difficult to get students to concentrate for more than an hour or two of others' presentations. Where classes are large, consider breaking the audience into groups, for example, dividing a class of 100 into four groups, with students presenting concurrently in different rooms, or at different timetabled slots.

7 **Think about the venue.** Students do not always give of their best in large, echoing tiered lecture theatres (nor do we!). A more intimate level class-room is less threatening, particularly for inexperienced presenters.

8 **Consider assessing using videotapes.** This can allow the presenters them-selves the opportunity to review their performances, and can allow you to assess presentations at a time most suitable to you. Viewing a selection of recorded presentations from earlier rounds can be useful for estab-lishing assessment criteria with students. This sort of evidence of teaching and learning is also useful to show external examiners.

9 **Start small.** Mini-presentations of one minute can be just as valuable as 20-minute presentations, especially as introductions to the task of standing up and addressing the peer-group.

10 **Check what other presentations students may be doing.** Sometimes it can seem that everyone is including presentations in their courses. If students find themselves giving three or four within a month or two, it can be very demanding on their time, and repetitious regarding the processes.

22

Assessing dissertations and theses

Students invest a great deal of time and energy in producing dissertations and theses. We therefore owe it to them to mark them fairly and appropriately. We address this below by listing some questions to ask about the process, and adding some suggestions.

1 **Are the assessment criteria explicit, clear, and understood by the students?** This may seem an obvious question. However, theses and dissertations are normally very different in the topics and themes they address, and the assessment criteria need to accommodate such differences. Students will naturally compare marks and feedback comments. The availability of clear criteria helps them see that their work has been assessed fairly.

2 **Get students to assess a few past dissertations.** You can't expect them to do this at the same level as may be appropriate for 'real' assessment, but you can (for example) issue students with a one-sided questionnaire to complete as they study examples of dissertations. Include questions about the power of the introduction, the quality and consistency of referencing, and the coherence of the conclusions.

3 **How can you offer guidance and support to students throughout the process?** Dissertations usually take students quite some time to complete. Students appreciate and require some help along the route. It is worth holding tutorials both individually and with groups. This takes good planning, and dates need to be set well in advance, and published on a notice board or handout to students.

4 **What student support mechanisms are available?** With large class sizes, we cannot afford to spend many hours of staff time with individual students. However, much valuable support can be drawn from the students themselves, if we facilitate ways of them helping each other. Consider introducing supplemental instruction processes, or setting up friendly yet critical student syndicates. Running a half-day workshop with students counselling each other can be valuable.

5 **How can you avoid bias?** Sometimes dissertations involve students writing on topics with a sensitive cultural or political nature. We need to be aware of any prejudices of our own, and to compensate for any bias these could cause in our assessment. Whenever possible, dissertations should be second-marked (at least!).

6 **Do all the students have equal opportunity regarding selecting their dissertation themes?** Research for some dissertations will involve students in visiting outside agencies, finding materials for experiments, building models and so on. With resource limitations becoming more severe, students may be forced to avoid certain topics altogether. Try to suggest topics where financial implications are manageable for students.

7 **Do dissertations always have to be bound?** This may depend on which year of the course they are set in. It may be worth reserving binding for final year dissertations, to help save students money.

8 **Help students to monitor their own progress.** It helps to map the assessment criteria in a way that helps students to keep track of their own progress and achievements. Computer programs are now available which help students work out how they are getting on, and prompt them to the next steps they should be considering at each stage.

9 **When assessing dissertations, collect a list of questions to select from at a forthcoming viva.** Even if there is not going to be a viva, such lists of questions can be a useful addition to the feedback you return to students.

10 **Use post-its while assessing dissertations and theses.** These can be placed towards the edges of pages, so that notes and questions written on the post-its can be found easily again. They help you avoid having to write directly on the pages of the dissertation or thesis and are especially useful with worries or questions that are addressed two pages later!

23

Assessing reviews and annotated bibliographies

In seeking to extend the range of methods by which we develop students' information retrieval skills, critical reviews of books and articles are frequently set as assignment tasks. Getting students to compile annotated bibliographies helps increase the breadth of their reading, and alerts them to sources they may not otherwise have seen. In assessing these forms of task, the following points are worth addressing.

1 **Promote variety.** Ask students to select their own subject for research, and give them a wide range of topics to choose from.

2 **Prompt awareness of audience.** Ask students to write reviews of different kinds of publication, so that they become aware of the differences in tone and style of writing which are appropriate for different audiences.

3 **Ask students to look at the same texts, but give them different focuses.** For example, students could look at a series of articles on pollution, and write several different reviews of them, aimed at conservationists, parents, individualists, and general consumers.

4 **Emphasise the importance of brevity.** It is much more difficult to write a concise pithy review than to ramble on with opinion and narrative at unspecified length. Short reviews are also quicker to mark (but make sure that students don't adopt the 'stop when you've written a thousand words' approach).

5 **Encourage qualitative judgement.** Prompt students to write on not only what a book or article is about, but also about how effective it is in providing convincing arguments, and how well it is expressed.

6   **Involve your library or information services staff.** It's a mean trick to send off groups of students to rampage through the library, without giving notice to the staff there of what you are doing. Discussing your plans with your faculty librarians, for example, gives them a chance to be prepared, and gives opportunities for them to make suggestions and give advice to you on the nature of the task, before you give it to students.

7   **Think hard about resource availability.** Make sure that there won't be severe log-jams with lots of students chasing particular library resources. Widen the range of suggested resources. Consider arranging with library staff that any books which will be in heavy demand are classified as 'reference only' stock for a specified period, so that they can remain in the library rather than disappearing on loan.

8   **Consider setting annotated bibliographies as group tasks.** This can encourage students to collaborate productively in future information seeking tasks, and can reduce the drudgery sometimes experienced in tasks such as literature searching.

9   **Make the final product 'publishable'.** Aim to compile collections of the best reviews and annotated bibliographies – for example, to use in next year's Course Handbook, or as the basis of an assessed task for next year's students.

10   **Consider delegating assessment to library staff (with their agreement!).** Library staff may be willing and able to assess annotated bibliographies and reviews with you, or may be willing to provide additional feedback comments to students.

24

Assessing performances

In many universities there are courses in subjects such as creative writing, dance, music, drama etc, where an element of performance is an integral part of the process. These elements are often regarded as more challenging to assess than, for example, written exams. The following suggestions may be helpful.

1 **Make sure the criteria for assessed performances are absolutely clear.** In the aesthetic domain, it is sometimes difficult to articulate these criteria without reducing them to absurdities. The key is to produce criteria that assess the essence of the performance rather than the easy-to-measure elements.

2 **Learn from the experience of others.** To develop expertise in assessing performances, it is invaluable to work alongside more experienced colleagues and learn from the ways in which they make evaluations or judgements.

3 **Ensure that the evidence of the elements of the performances is recorded.** Use video, audiotape, notation or other methods, so there is evidence available for moderation subsequently.

4 **Stage assessment over a period of time.** It is often helpful to have an incremental element to the assessment so that 'work in progress' assessed at intermediate points contributes to the final grade.

5 **Require students to keep careful records of their preparations for the performances.** This makes it possible for their reflections on the processes, by which their performances were developed, to contribute to their assessment.

6 **Include peer-assessment.** Students on a course can contribute to the assessment of each other's performances, so long as the assessment criteria are explicit, and evidence of successful outcomes is required. Intra-group assessment can also be helpful, for example with students who are performing together in a play or dance performance.

7 **Minimise competition.** Students in the performing arts move in a competitive world, and assessment schemes which prioritise 'the best' and 'winning' can be counter-productive in contexts where peer support and peer-assessment are interdependent.

8 **Use audiences to contribute to the assessment.** Performances often provide excellent opportunities for gaining a range of views of achievement. Beware, however, of candidates packing audiences with their fans and friends, and devise criteria that are quantifiable as well as qualitative.

9 **Accommodate issues relating to style and personal taste.** Where there are such issues in play, assessors should make these explicit at the outset. This will at least provide information to enable students to make choices about how they prefer to perform.

10 **Be aware of the stresses that performances can put on candidates.** In addition to the performance anxiety that is common in most kinds of assessment, there are further stresses that can occur. Examples include when scenery falls, instruments get damaged, audiovisual equipment fails, and injuries befall performers. Aim to develop styles of assessment that can accommodate glitches, and ensure that such happenings don't necessarily indicate failure.

25

Assessing poster displays and exhibitions

Asking students (individually or in groups) to synthesise the outcomes of their learning and/or research into a self-explanatory poster, which can be assessed on the spot, can be an extremely valuable process. More and more conferences are providing poster display opportunities as an effective way of disseminating findings and ideas. This kind of assessment can be good practice for developing the skills relevant to communicating by such visual means.

1 **Use the assessment process as a showcase.** Students are often rather proud of their achievements and it can be invaluable to invite others in to see what has been achieved. Think about inviting moderators, senior staff, students on parallel courses, and employers. Gather their impressions, either using a short questionnaire, or verbally asking them a couple of relevant questions about their experiences of seeing the display.

2 **Use posters as a way to help other students to learn.** For example, final year students can produce posters showing the learning they gained during placements. This can be a useful opportunity for students, who are preparing to find their own placements, to adjust their approaches and base them on others' experiences.

3 **Get students to peer-assess each other's posters.** Having undertaken the task of making posters themselves, they will be well prepared to review critically the work of others. This also provides chances for them to learn from the research undertaken by the whole class rather than just from their own work.

4 **Consider asking students to produce a one-page handout to supplement their poster.** This will test a further set of skills, and will provide all reviewers with an *aide mémoire* for subsequent use.

5 **Give sufficient time for the debrief.** Lots of learning takes place in the discussion during and after the display. The tendency is to put on poster display and exhibition sessions during the last week of the term or semester, and this can give little time to unpack the ideas at the end.

6 **Make careful practical arrangements.** Large numbers of posters take up a lot of display space, and to get the best effect they should be displayed on boards. Organising this is possible in most universities, for example, by borrowing publicity display boards, but it needs to be planned in advance. Allow sufficient time for students to mount their displays, and make available drawing pins, Blu-Tack, tape, Velcro sticky pads, dismantleable display equipment, etc.

7 **Stagger the assessment.** Where peers are assessing each other's posters, to avoid collusion, 'fixing', and outbursts of spite, it is valuable to arrange that half the display is in one room and the rest in another, or to run successive displays at different times. Number the posters and get one half of the group to assess the odd-numbered posters and the other half to assess the even-numbered ones, and average the data which are produced.

8 **Consider getting groups to produce a poster between them.** This encourages collaborative working and can reduce the overall numbers of posters – useful when student numbers are large. You could then consider getting students within the group to peer-assess (intra) their respective contributions to the group as well as to assess collaboratively the posters of the other groups (inter-peer-group assessment).

9 **Link assessment of poster displays to open days.** Students coming to visit the institution when they are considering applying for courses may well get a good idea about what students actually do on the courses, from looking at posters on display.

10 **Prepare a suitable assessment sheet.** Base this firmly on the assessment criteria for the exercise. Provide space for peers' comments. This paves the way towards plenty of opportunity for peer feedback.

11 **Use assistance.** When working with large numbers of peer-assessed posters, you may need help in working out the average scores. Either get the students to do the number work for themselves or for each other (and advise them that the numbers will be randomly checked to ensure fair play). In fact, there is usually less chance of mistakes when students do the number work than when teachers do it themselves! Alternatively, press-gang colleagues, partners, administrators, or progeny to help with the task.

12 **Provide a rehearsal opportunity.** Let the students have a practice run at a relatively early stage, using a mock-up or a draft on flipchart paper. Give them feedback on these drafts, and let them compare their ideas. This can help them to avoid the most obvious disasters later.

13 **Let everyone know why they are using poster displays.** This method of assessment may be unfamiliar to students, and to your colleagues. It is therefore valuable if you can provide a clear justification of the educational merits of the method to all concerned.

14 **Brief students really carefully about what is needed.** Ideally, let them see a whole range of posters from previous years (or some mock-ups, or photographs of previous displays) so that they have a good idea about the requirements, without having their originality and creativity suppressed.

15 **Use the briefing to discuss criteria and weighting.** Students will need to know what level of effort they should put into different elements such as presentation, information content, structure, visual features, and so on. If students are not clear about this, you may well end up with brilliantly presented posters with little relevance to the topic, or really dull, dense posters that try to compress the whole text of a long report onto a single A1 sheet.

16 **Give students some practical guidelines.** Let them know how many A1 sheets they can have, where their work will be displayed, what size of font the text should be to be readable on a poster, what resources will be available to them in college, and how much help they can get from outsiders such as friends on other courses who take good photographs or who have the knack of writing in attractive script.

17 **Attach a budget to the task.** In poster displays, money shows! If you were to give a totally free hand to students, the ones with best access to photocopiers, photographic resources, expensive papers, word processors and so on may well produce better looking products than students who have little money to spend on their posters or displays (although it does not always turn out this way). Giving a notional budget can help to even out the playing field, as can requiring students to only use items from a given list, with materials perhaps limited to those provided in workshops in the college.

18 **Keep records of poster displays and exhibitions.** Take photographs, or make a short video. It is not possible to retain complete displays and exhibitions, but a handy reminder can be very useful when planning the next similar event. Evidence of the displays can also be interesting to external examiners and quality assessors.

19 **Get someone (or a group) to provide a 'guide booklet' to the exhibition.** This helps the students undertaking this task to make relative appraisals of the different items or collections making up the exhibition as a whole.

20 **Consider turning it into a celebration as well.** After the assessment has taken place, it can be pleasurable to provide some refreshments, and make the display or exhibition part of an end-of-term or end-of-course celebration.

26

Assessing laboratory work

In many subjects, some of the most important learning occurs in laboratories, and in associated work done before and after practical sessions. It is important to try to assess this learning carefully. The following suggestions may help your students get the most out of such work.

1 **Give clear guidance regarding the format of reports.** For example, issue a sheet listing principal generic section headings, with a short description of the purpose and nature of each main section in a typical report.

2 **Get students to assess subjectively some past reports.** Issue students with copies of some good, bad and indifferent reports, and ask them to mark them independently, simply giving each example an impression mark. Then facilitate a discussion where students explain why they allocated the marks in the ways they did.

3 **Get students to assess objectively some past reports.** Issue groups of students with good, bad and indifferent reports, along with a sheet listing assessment criteria and a mark scheme. Ask each group to assess the reports. Then initiate discussions and comparisons between groups.

4 **Publish clear deadlines for the submission of successive reports.** Allow only one or two weeks after the laboratory session; it is kinder to students to get them to write-up early, rather than to allow them to accumulate a backlog of report writing, which can interfere (for example) with their revision for exams.

5 **Don't insist on full reports too often.** Issue briefings for short-form reports, and, for example, allow students to be assessed on any three full reports and any six short-form reports out of twelve laboratory sessions.

6 **Prepare a standard assessment/feedback grid, to return to students with marked reports.** Include criteria and marks associated with quality of data, observations, calculations, conclusions, references and verdicts.

7 **Allocate practical work in advance of the sessions, and include some assessed pre-laboratory preparation.** For example, pose half-a-dozen short-answer questions for students to complete before starting a piece of laboratory work. This helps students know what they are doing, rather than follow instructions blindly. It also avoids wasting time at the start of a laboratory session working out which students are prepared to undertake each experiment.

8 **Include in examinations some questions linked closely to laboratory work.** For example, tell students that two exam questions will be based on work they will have done in the laboratory. This helps to ensure that lab work isn't forgotten when students start revising for exams.

9 **Get students to design exam questions based on laboratory work.** Set groups of students this task. Allocate some marks for the creativity of their questions. When done over several years, the results could be turned into a bank of questions which could be placed on computer for students to consult as they prepared for exams.

10 **Consider the use of computers in the laboratory.** Where facilities are available, arrange that students can input their experimental data directly onto a computer or network. Many universities now enable students to write up their reports straight into a word processor alongside the laboratory bench, using a report template on disk. Such reports can be handed in immediately at the end of the laboratory session, and marked and returned promptly.

27

Assessing practical work

Practical skills are important in many subject areas. This importance is often reflected by the time students spend in laboratories, workshops, and other situations where they practise and develop such skills. However, it is worth asking whether we are actually measuring these skills directly, or whether we are only managing to measure the final products of the application of such skills. Addressing the following questions may be beneficial in our efforts to get the balance right.

1 **What exactly are the practical skills we wish to assess?** These may include a vast range of important skills, from deftness in assembling complex glassware in a chemistry laboratory to precision and speed in using a scalpel on the operating table. It is important that students know the relative importance of each skill.

2 **Why do we need to measure practical skills?** The credibility of our courses often depends on what students can do when they enter employment. It is often said by employers that students are very knowledgeable, but not necessarily competent in practical tasks.

3 **Where is the best place to try to measure these skills?** Sometimes practical skills can be measured in places such as laboratories or workshops. For other skills, students may need to be working in real-life situations.

4 **When is the best time to measure practical skills?** When practical skills are vitally important, it is probably best to start measuring them very early on in a course, so that any students showing alarming problems with them can be appropriately advised or redirected.

5 **Who is in the best position to measure practical skills?** For many practical skills, the only valid way of measuring them involves someone making detailed observations while students demonstrate the skills involved. This can be very time-consuming if it has to be done by staff, and also can feel very threatening to students.

6 **Is it necessary to establish minimum acceptable standards?** In many jobs, it is quite essential that everyone practising does so with a high level of skill (for example, surgery!). In other situations, it is possible to agree on a reasonable level of skills, and for this to be safe enough (for example, teaching!).

7 **How much should practical skills count for?** Students often spend a considerable proportion of their time developing and practising practical skills. It is important to think clearly about what contribution to their overall assessment such skills should make, and to let students know this.

8 **Is student self-assessment of practical skills worth using?** Getting students to assess their own practical skills can be one way round the impossible workloads which could be involved if staff were to do all the requisite observations. It is much quicker for staff to moderate student self-assessment of such skills than to undertake the whole task of assessing them.

9 **Is student peer-assessment of practical skills worth using?** Involving students in peer-assessment of practical skills can be much less threatening than using tutor assessment. The act of assessing a peer's practical skills is often very good for peer-assessors, in terms of improving similar skills of their own.

10 **Is it necessary to have a practical examination?** In some subjects, some sort of end-point test may be deemed essential. Driving tests, for example, could not be solely replaced by a written examination on the Highway Code.

28

Assessing students in seminars

Assessing students in seminars can add to the diversity of assessment methods, and allow for instant feedback, providing a valuable learning experience. As seminar groups are smaller than lecture groups, it is possible to employ some different assessment methods. The following suggestions may help your students derive more benefit from seminars.

1 **Brainstorm assessment possibilities with students.** Get groups of students to draw up lists of the possible ways their seminars could be assessed. Collect and collate the contents of the lists, and ask the whole group to vote on the three best ways.

2 **Get students to identify criteria by which to assess seminars.** For example, show a video of a previous seminar and ask the students first to give it an impression rating. Then help them identify some objective criteria that could be used to assess it, and which also could be extended to assess their own forthcoming seminars.

3 **Prepare a seminar of your own, and get students to assess it.** Try to include in your seminar the good practice features that you wish students to emulate. Be prepared, however, to learn some home truths about your own performance, and don't get cross when you receive critical comments!

4 **Get students themselves to peer-assess seminars.** Ask small groups of students to organise and prepare a seminar. Keep the presentations short and snappy (not a whole hour each!). Get the whole group to write assessment criteria, and decide on the relative weightings for these, and draw up assessment sheets using these. Allow the groups to assess each other's presentation (inter-peer-group assessment). You could try as a first stage getting students to give marks on two aspects of each seminar – content and presentation – and use number cards as in ice skating or ballroom dancing competitions.

5 **Use the time carefully.** Getting students to plan the organisation of both the seminars and the assessment can enable the timetabled sessions to be used effectively.

6 **Consider assessing small tasks within the seminar.** For example, ask all students attending the seminar to write an article on the topic under discussion for a newspaper. Collect the articles and distribute them. The individual marks for the articles can contribute towards the seminar assessment mark.

7 **Get students to write their own reflective logs about their contributions to the seminar programme.** Get the students to self-assess these logs. Students are remarkably honest about how well they feel they have contributed, although they will probably need some briefing and support regarding how to assess themselves.

8 **Keep records of students' interactions, and give them grades for them.** At its simplest, this means that a student who failed to attend a sufficient proportion of the seminars would be deemed to have failed the seminar element of the overall assessment programme. More sophisticated systems would allow you to differentiate students in terms of pass, merit or distinction, based on criteria you made public to the students at the outset. If you do this, it is important to make it clear that 'hogging the air' does not constitute good performance, whereas 'enabling the contribution of others' does.

9 **Use parallel seminar groups to assess each other's presentations.** This can take time to set up, but enables students to learn from each other, particularly when different seminar topics are given.

10 **Get students in seminars to include reviews of journal articles.** This can help them develop similar skills to those needed to produce book reviews, but takes less time, and can be assessed within the seminar sessions.

Chapter 6 Traditional Exams And Vivas

We have already indicated our belief that traditional forms of assessment are over-employed in many courses in higher education, and our view that while these forms of assessment may be highly objective at measuring some things, they may be measuring too limited a range of aspects of learning. We also believe that much can be done to make traditional forms of assessment work rather better than they often do, and in this chapter we give our suggestions.

The quality of traditional exams rests on the quality of the questions that they contain. Therefore, we start by offering advice to those designing and writing such questions, especially those doing so for the first time. Closely connected to question design is the production of a matching marking scheme, and we continue with suggestions about how these can be made sufficiently good to be explicit to students and the outside world.

There is growing recognition that many forms of traditional exam favour those students who happen to be skilled at doing traditional exams! However, an important factor in this state of affairs is that often students know little about how exam questions are marked by examiners. One of the best ways of improving this situation is to use exam questions as the basis for class exercises, and share the hidden agendas.

We follow our discussion of traditional exams with some suggestions about how students who have failed can be helped. Failure can be a very traumatic experience for students, and can damage their motivation to learn so much that they effectively stop in their tracks.

We end this chapter with some recommendations about another form of traditional assessment: the viva. Vivas can be very useful opportunities to test things that can't be tested adequately on the basis of written performance. However, as each viva is an individual event (and a very important one to the students involved), it is necessary to reflect on our approaches to setting these up, implementing them, and debriefing students after them.

29

Setting traditional exam questions

Setting exams always seems to be required at the last moment at short notice! Yet this is one of the most important tasks lecturers ever do (and is probably far more important than teaching!). The words you choose when setting questions will have far-reaching effects on the lives and careers of students. The following suggestions may help you to choose your words carefully, and check them thoroughly.

1 **Set questions that seek to discover what has been learned, rather than what has been taught.** Avoid testing basic information recall, and try to set questions which require students to make use of their knowledge, and to re-interpret it intelligently.

2 **Keep the language simple.** Students have enough to cope with in the terror and stress of exam conditions, without having to cope with linguistic and syntactical complexity!

3 **Make the rubric unambiguous.** More students fail exams because they do not follow the instructions on number of questions and length of answers, than through lack of knowledge. Try your paper out on a 'naive reader' (rather than on a colleague who knows the form), and see if it is easy to understand exactly what the rubric is instructing candidates to do.

4 **Avoid trick questions.** Such questions tend to demonstrate the cleverness of the examiner rather than the true worth of the students. Exams should always aim to test ability fairly, rather than to play games with students.

5 **When setting questions, think about what students would need to do to answer them effectively.** Prepare your marking brief at the same time. Even open ended questions should be written with a clear view of what would constitute evidence of successful achievement.

6 **Consider making the mark scheme explicit.** When students can see details of the marking scheme on the question paper, they can spend more time on the parts of the exam that carry most marks, and avoid wasting a lot of time on less important areas.

7 **Don't expect students to write too much.** While word limits can provide useful guidance in continuous assessment, in exams, unrealistic word-length guidance can cause extra and unnecessary stress.

8 **Take into account that many students don't write well or quickly by hand any more.** Many students nowadays work mostly on wordprocessors, and find the process of writing by hand slow and unwieldy, with no opportunities for on-line editing. This may be the main cause of some work that looks scrappy or full of amendments on scripts.

9 **Be creative.** Think about the possibility of allowing students to write one question of their own in an exam, and even a marking scheme for it, then answer it. It is obviously harder to mark the range of totally different products such a process gives, but it allows students to demonstrate their strengths.

10 **Ask one or two colleagues to paraphrase or summarise your exam questions.** Maybe choose one colleague who knows the subject well, and one from a different area. Look at how their wording differs from yours, and decide which version or combination may be the most appropriate to use.

30

Writing marking schemes

Making a good marking scheme can save you hours when it comes to marking a pile of answers. It can also help you to know that you are doing everything possible to be uniformly fair to all students. In addition, your marking schemes will normally be shown to people, including external examiners and maybe quality assessors, so it's important to do it well. The following suggestions should help.

1 **Write a model answer for each question.** This can be a useful first step towards identifying the mark-bearing ingredients of a good answer. It also helps you see when what you thought was going to be a 30-minute question turns out to take an hour! If you have difficulties answering the questions, the chances are that your students will too! Making model answers and marking schemes for coursework assignments can give you good practice for writing exam schemes.

2 **Make each decision as straightforward as possible.** Try to allocate each mark so that it is associated with something that is either there or absent, or right or wrong.

3 **Aim to make the scheme usable by a non-expert in the subject.** This can help your marking schemes be useful resources for students themselves, perhaps in next year's course.

4 **Aim to make it so that anyone can mark answers, and agree on the scores within a mark or two.** It is best to involve colleagues in your piloting of first-draft marking schemes. They will soon help you to identify areas where the marking criteria may need clarifying or tightening up.

5 **Allow for 'consequential' marks.** For example, when a candidate makes an early mistake, but then proceeds correctly thereafter (especially in problems and calculations), allow for marks to be given for the correct steps even when the final answer is quite wrong.

6 **Pilot a marking scheme by showing it to others.** It's worth even showing marking schemes to people who are not closely associated with your subject area. If they can't see exactly what you're looking for, it may be that the scheme is not yet sufficiently self-explanatory. Extra detail you then add may help you to clarify your own thinking, and will certainly assist fellow markers.

7 **Make yourself think about honourable exceptions.** Ask yourself whether your marking scheme is sufficiently flexible to accommodate a brilliant student who hasn't strictly conformed to your original idea of what should be achieved. There are sometimes candidates who write exceptionally good answers which are off-beat and idiosyncratic, and they deserve credit for these.

8 **Consider having more than 20 marks for a 20-mark question.** Especially in essay-type answers, you can't expect students to include all the things you may think of yourself. It may be worth having up to 30 or more 'available' marks, so that students approaching the question in different ways still have the opportunity to score well.

9 **Look at what others have done in the past.** If it's your first time writing a marking scheme, looking at other people's ways of doing them will help you to focus your efforts. Choose to look at marking schemes from other subjects that your students may be studying, to help you tune in to the assessment culture of the course.

10 **Learn from your own mistakes.** Keep a note of any difficulties you experience in marking your own scheme, and take account of these next time you have to prepare one. You won't stop making mistakes altogether, but at least you'll make different mistakes!

31

Marking traditional exams

The following suggestions may help you approach the task of marking exam scripts efficiently and in a way that is helpful to students.

1 **Be realistic about what you can do.** Marking scripts can be boring, exhausting and stressful. As far as constraints allow, don't attempt to mark large numbers of scripts in short periods of time. Put scripts for marking into manageable bundles. It is less awesome to have ten scripts on your desk and the rest out of sight than to have the whole pile threatening you as you work.

2 **Avoid halo effects.** If you've just marked a brilliant answer on a script, it can be easy to go into the same student's next answer seeing only the good points and passing over the weaknesses. Try to ensure that you mark each answer dispassionately.

3 **Watch out for prejudices.** There will be all sorts of things you like and dislike about the style and layout of scripts, not to mention handwriting quality. Make sure that each time there is a 'benefit of the doubt' decision to be made, it is not influenced by such factors.

4 **Recognise that your mood will change.** Every now and then, check back to scripts you marked earlier, and see whether your generosity has increased or decreased. Be aware of the middle-mark bunching syndrome. As you get tired, it is safe and easy to give a middle-range mark. Try as far as possible to look at each script afresh.

5 **Remind yourself of the importance of what you're doing.** You may be marking a whole pile of scripts, but each individual script may be a crucial landmark in the life and career of the student concerned. Your verdict may affect students for the rest of their careers.

6 **Take account of the needs of second markers.** Many universities use a blind double marking system, in which case you should not make any written comments or numbers on the scripts themselves, to avoid prejudicing the judgment of a second marker. You may find it useful to use post-its or assessment forms for each script, so you are able to justify the marks you give at any later stage. Such *aides mémoire* can save you having to read the scripts again, rethinking how you arrived at your numbers or grades.

7 **Write feedback for students.** In most exams, the system may not allow you to write on the scripts the sort of feedback you would have given if the questions had been set as assessed coursework. However, students still need feedback, and making notes of the things you would have explained about common mistakes can help you prepare some discussion notes to issue to students after the exam, or can remind you of things to mention next time you teach the same subjects.

8 **Devise your own system.** You may prefer to mark a whole script or just Question 1 of every script first. Do what you feel comfortable with, and see what works best for you.

9 **Provide feedback for yourself and for the course team.** As you work through the scripts, note how many students answered each question, and how well they performed. You may begin to realise that some questions turned out to have been very well written, while others could have been framed better. Such feedback and reflection should prove very useful when designing questions for next time round.

10 **Set aside time for a review.** Having marked all the scripts, you may wish to capture your thoughts, such as suggestions about changes for part of the course or module, or the processes used to teach it.

32

Using exam questions as class exercises

Answering exam questions is still the principal skill that students need to succeed in higher education. In our attempts to increase the learning payoff of taught sessions, we can help students to develop their exam skills by making use of exam questions. The following suggestions may help you build related activities into lectures and tutorials.

1 **Let a class have a try at an exam question under exam conditions.** Then ask students to exchange their answers, and lead them through the marking using a typical marking scheme. This helps students to learn quickly how examiners' minds work.

2 **Issue two or three old exam questions for students to try in preparation for a tutorial.** Then lead them through the assessment during the tutorial. Ask them to prepare lists of questions on matters arising from the exercise, both on subject content and requirements for exams, and use these questions to focus tutorial discussion.

3 **Display an exam question on screen in a large group lecture.** Ask students in groups to brainstorm the principal steps they would take in the way they would approach answering the question. Then give out a model answer to the question as a handout, and talk the class through the points where marks were earned.

4 **In a lecture or a tutorial, get students in groups to think up exam questions themselves.** You can base this on work they have already covered, or on work currently in progress. Ask the groups to transcribe their questions onto overhead transparencies. Display each of these in turn, giving feedback on how appropriate or otherwise each question is in terms of standard, wording, length and structure. (You will get many questions this way which you can later use or adapt!)

5 **Use exam questions to help students to create an agenda.** In a lecture or tutorial, give out two or three related exam questions as a handout. Ask students in groups to make lists of short questions that they don't yet know the answers to. Then allow the groups to use you as a resource, quizzing you with these questions. You don't have to answer them all at once – for some your reply will be along the lines of 'We'll come to this in a week or two', and for others 'You won't actually be required to know this'.

6 **Get students to make marking schemes.** Give them a typical exam question, and ask groups of students to prepare a breakdown of how they think the marks should be allocated. Ask them to transcribe the marking schemes to overhead transparencies. Discuss each of these in turn with the whole group, and give guidance to how closely the marking schemes resemble those used in practice.

7 **Get students to surf the net.** Ask them to access the Internet to see if they can find appropriate exam questions on the subjects they are studying. Suggest that they work in twos or threes, and bring the questions they find to the next class session. You can encourage them to download the questions they find, and make an electronic question bank.

8 **Ask students in groups to think up a 'dream' question.** Ask the groups to make bullet-point lists of the ten most important things that they would include in answers to these questions. These questions will give you useful information about their favourite topics.

9 **Ask students in groups to think up 'nightmare' questions.** With these, you can open up a discussion of the causes of their anxieties and traumas, and can probably do a lot to allay their fears, and point them in the right direction regarding how they might tackle such questions.

10 **Ask students to think of way-out, alternative questions.** Suggest that they think of questions which are just as testing of their knowledge and skills as 'normal' questions, but which get them to think laterally and creatively. This encourages deeper reflection about the material they are learning, and will probably give you some interesting ideas to use in future exams.

33

Helping students cope with exam failure

Of course, we'd all prefer that such help was not needed. However, in most exam systems, casualties seem inevitable. The fact that some students did not pass does not mean that they could not pass. The following suggestions may help you to prepare students who failed for future successes.

1 **Help students to come to a position where they can see failure as an opportunity for learning.** This is better than the natural instinct which leads people to regard failure as a major disaster. Failing an exam can be a strong demotivator, but it can also be an opportunity to seek feedback, providing a stimulus for deeper learning.

2 **Take account of the feelings of students.** Students who fail exams often take it as a blow to their self-esteem. Be prepared for a whole range of resultant emotions, including anger, inertia, disbelief, and inconsolable grief. For students who have done well at school, failing exams at university may be their first experiences of failure, and may give them a profound shock. For those who struggled to get to university, exam failure may confirm their underlying thoughts that they were never quite up to it in the first place.

3 **Concentrate on what students can do in future to improve, rather than railing over their failings.** Let students see a range of examples of satisfactory and good work (rather than just model answers, which imply the need for perfection).

4 **Let students have further opportunities for practising under simulated exam conditions.** Ideally, this can give students the chance to experience success before they next experience real exams.

5 **When possible, keep students who have failed exams in touch with others in the same situation.** This helps them not to feel isolated in their failure. Promote and encourage self-help groups where possible, so students can motivate and support each other.

6 **Let students play examiner.** Give students the chance to apply assessment schemes to examples of good, bad and indifferent exam scripts (and, if possible, to their own scripts which failed). Such a process rapidly increases students' awareness of the rules of the exam game.

7 **Give students opportunities to reflect on unsuccessful exam performance.** Allow time to identify what they could have done to prepare for the exam more effectively, and how their performance on the day may have been approached more successfully.

8 **Help students to identify what went well.** Even in a failed exam, most students display strengths in some parts of some questions. Help them not do dismiss these strengths in the context of their overall failure, and encourage them to extend the areas of success on future occasions.

9 **Help students develop revision and exam techniques.** There are plenty of books, learning packages and computer packages available to help students build up confidence.

10 **Encourage students in pairs to set each other questions and mark them.** Informally talking through their answers to each other can motivate them, and help them improve their self-confidence.

34

Conducting a viva

Vivas are used for a variety of purposes, and with varying degrees of importance. The following suggestions may help you prepare yourself for conducting vivas, as well as helping your students have a better experience of them.

1 **Decide what the viva is for.** For example, the agenda could range from confirming that the candidates did indeed do the work represented in their dissertations, to proving whether their understanding of the subject reached acceptable levels.

2 **Prepare your students for vivas.** Explain to them what a viva is, and what they will normally be expected to do. It helps to give them opportunities to practise. Much of this they can do on their own, but they will need you to start them off on the right lines, and to check now and then that their practice sessions are realistic.

3 **Think about the room layout.** Sitting the candidate on a hard seat while you and your fellow-assessors sit face-on behind a large table is guaranteed to make the candidate tremble! If possible, sit beside or close to the candidate. Where appropriate provide students with a table on which to put any papers they may have with them.

4 **Think about the waiting room.** If candidates are queuing together for long, they can make each other even more nervous. If you're asking the same questions of a series of students, the word will get around about what you're asking.

5 **Prepare yourself for vivas!** Normally, if you're a principal player at a viva, you will have read the student's work in some detail. It helps if you come to the viva armed with a list of questions you may ask. You don't have to ask all of them, but it helps to have some ready! Normally, you will need to have a pre-viva discussion with other members of the examining panel, and you need to be seen to have done your homework.

6 **Do your best to put the candidate at ease.** Students find vivas very stressful, and it improves their confidence and fluency if they are greeted cheerily and made welcome at the start of a viva.

7 **When vivas are a formality, indicate this.** When students have done well on the written side of their work, and it's fairly certain that they should pass, it helps to give a strong hint about this straightaway. It puts students at ease, and makes for a more interesting and relaxed viva.

8 **Ask open questions which enable students to give full and articulate answers.** Try to avoid questions which lead to minimal or 'yes/no' replies.

9 **Let students do most of the talking.** The role of an examiner in a viva is to provoke thought and prompt candidates into speaking fluently about the work or topics under discussion, and to spark off an intellectual dialogue. It is not to harangue, carp or demonstrate the examiner's intelligence, or to trick candidates!

10 **Give students feedback on their vivas.** Sometimes it may be necessary for the examining panel to have a short private discussion to reach a decision or to check that what everyone seems to think is a foregone conclusion is indeed unanimous. Whatever the decision, it is useful for students if you can tell them a little about the strengths and weaknesses they displayed.

35

Debriefing after a viva

Vivas can be very useful learning experiences, but much of the experience can be lost if time is not set aside for a debrief. Such debriefing is particularly useful when students will encounter vivas again. We suggest some ways of going about this.

1   **Write your own notes during each viva.** If you are dealing with a series of such events, it can become difficult to remember each feedback point that you want to give to each student.

2   **Consider recording vivas on video.** This is particularly worthwhile when one of your main aims is to prepare students for more important vivas to follow. Simply allowing students to borrow the recordings and look at them in the comfort of privacy can provide students with useful deep reflection on their performance. It is sometimes more comfortable to view the recordings in the atmosphere of a supportive student group.

3   **Ask students to write reflections afterwards.** Suggest that this should be no more than one page. Ask them to think about what went especially well and what they would now modify in the light of experience if doing the same viva again. It is useful to show reflections made by previous students (with their permission).

4   **Tell students in advance that there will be a debriefing.** This can take some of the strain away from students, when they know that they will be able to get advice and feedback on any areas they found difficult.

5   **Ask students for their opinions first.** This can spare them the embarrassment of you telling them about failings they already know they have. You may also find useful food for thought when students tell you about aspects of the vivas that you were unaware of yourself.

6 **Be sensitive.** Vivas can be traumatic for students, and they may have put much time and effort into preparing for them. Choose words carefully, particularly when giving feedback on aspects which were unsuccessful.

7 **Be specific.** Students will naturally want to have feedback on details of things they did particularly well. As far as you can, make sure you can find something positive to say even when overall performance was not good.

8 **Run a role-play afterwards.** Ask students to play both examiners and candidates, and bring to life some of the issues they encountered in their vivas. This can allow other students observing the role-play to think about aspects they did not experience themselves.

9 **Plan for the next step.** Get students to discuss strategies for preparing for their next viva, and ask groups of students to make lists of 'dos and don'ts' to bear in mind next time.

10 **Get students to produce a guidance booklet about preparing for vivas and taking part in them.** This may be useful for future students, but is equally valuable to the students making it, as a way of getting them to consolidate their reflections on their own experience.

Chapter 7 Multiple Choice Questions And Responses

In this short chapter, we concentrate on a different sort of testing: that based on the decision-making skills used in picking the best option from a set of alternatives. Multiple choice questions can be used to test a wide range of knowledge and understanding. In fact, since such testing does not involve students having to write out what they know long hand, it is possible to test a much wider agenda in an hour than would be possible in written exams.

We start with some suggestions about the design of multiple choice questions. It is important that such questions are designed with considerable care, and that they are piloted well before being used in any formal testing.

Multiple choice questions are an excellent way of giving learners vital feedback on their learning. In particular, when they choose an incorrect option, it is possible to design feedback responses which allow them to find out not only what the correct option should have been, but also what was wrong with the option chosen. Once designed, multiple choice questions and feedback responses can be packaged, either in print or using computer-based formats, allowing both the testing and feedback to take place without using staff time.

We end this chapter with ideas about using multiple choice questions in exam modes. Again, we suggest that the opportunity for providing students with feedback on their performance should not be missed.

36

Writing multiple choice questions

A multiple choice question has three main ingredients: the 'stem', which sets the context, the 'key', which is the best option or the correct one, and 'distractors', which are options containing faults or errors. The following suggestions should help you to get all three parts of multiple choice questions working effectively.

1 **Make sure that the key is definitely correct!** It should not be possible for students to find anything wrong or arguable in the key.

2 **Make sure that the key does not stand out for the wrong reasons as being correct.** The key should not be given away by containing leading wording from the stem, nor should it be of significantly different length than the other options. Also make sure that any grammar links between the stem and the key don't give the key away.

3 **Take care with 'definites' versus 'indefinites'.** It is alright to have sets of options including indefinite words such as 'sometimes, often, usually, rarely' *or* definite words such as 'always, never, all, none' but it is not wise to combine the two kinds of words in a given question, as the indefinite options are more likely to be chosen as correct by anyone who is just guessing – and probably are correct too!

4 **Make sure that the stem provides a clear task.** For example, be clear about whether 'which...?' means 'which *one*...?' or 'which (one or more)...?' It is best to avoid options such as 'all of these' or 'none of these'. These tend to be chosen as cop-out selections by candidates who are not thinking deeply enough to identify the best option.

5 **Be careful with negative questions.** For example, if asking 'which one of the following is *not* true?' or 'which is an *exception* to the rule?', make it really stand out that it is a 'wrong' option that has to be selected in such questions; candidates become accustomed to looking for correct options.

6 **Make sure that there is something wrong with each distractor.** Remember that when you write a feedback response to a distractor you need to be able to explain convincingly what is wrong with it, or why the key is better.

7 **Choose distractors which represent likely errors.** There is no point in having distractors which are not chosen as 'correct' by at least someone! Distractors need to be as plausible as you can make them.

8 **Let students help you to find better distractors.** It is worth posing the stem as an open-ended question to a class, and finding out what the most common wrong answers are. These can then form the basis of your distractors.

9 **Try questions out on a large group.** For example, in a lecture put the question up on the screen, and ask for a show of hands for each option in turn. When everyone chooses the correct (or best) option, your distractors may need to be made a bit more appealing!

10 **Remember that multiple choice questions are not restricted to simple formats.** For example, an extended set of options can be used, with the question asking students to decide which *combination* of options is correct or best (for example 'a, d, e' or 'b, c, e' etc).

37

Writing feedback responses to multiple choice questions

Whatever form your multiple choice questions take (print-based learning package, computer-based package, or multiple choice test), learners want (and need) to find out two things every time they make a choice: 'Was I right?' and 'if not, *why* not'. The following suggestions may help your responses provide useful, quick feedback to learners.

1 **Think about when your response will be seen.** For example, learners may see your response immediately on-screen after picking an option in a computer-based package, or they may see it in print after completing a series of questions in a multiple choice test.

2 **Make it immediately clear whether the option was correct or not.** Instant feedback can be very useful, particularly when you can remind students of why they were right, or show them why they were wrong.

3 **Give appropriate praise for the choice of correct options.** A few well-chosen words can be encouraging for learners who made the correct choice.

4 **Make sure that 'well done' messages don't get boring or out of control!** There are hundreds of ways of responding 'well done'. Save the 'splendid!' responses for right answers to really tricky questions. Milder forms of 'well done' include 'yes', 'right', 'of course'.

5 **Respond to learners who choose distractors.** It's little use just saying to them 'wrong, the correct option was A'. Learners want (and need) to find out why the distractor was not the best option. If you can't respond to a distractor, take it as a sign that it was not a good distractor in the first place. Good distractors are wrong for a reason, not just wrong!

6 **Acknowledge learners who choose options that are partly correct.** When part of a distractor is correct, use words to remind learners who have chosen it that they did indeed have some good reasons for their choices. For example, 'while it is true to say that..., however it is not true to conclude that...'.

7 **Treat learners choosing distractors gently.** Don't leave them feeling that they must be the only people ever to have made such mistakes. Words like 'this was a tricky question', or 'most people find this hard at first' can go a long way towards making it more acceptable to choose distractors.

8 **Give learners the opportunity to give you feedback on your feedback.** Check particularly that when you explain what was wrong with distractors, learners get your messages clearly.

9 **Think of visual ways of responding.** Some learners may wish to be responded to visually rather than with words – at least sometimes. Try to arrange coffee with a computer-graphics expert if you're designing responses for a computer-based package.

10 **Keep the language of responses familiar and friendly.** Responses should address the student as 'you' and should use simple, accessible vocabulary. A sense of humour usually helps, but excessive humour (especially of feeble puns) can be counter-productive!

38

Designing multiple choice exams

When multiple choice questions are used for exams rather than just for self-assessment, feedback or diagnostic testing, much more care needs to be taken regarding the design and validation of the questions. The following suggestions may help you to devise effective multiple choice exams.

1 **Check the performance of each question with large numbers of students before including it in an exam.** The most suitable questions are those which discriminate between the able and less able candidates. There are statistical packages which can help you work out the 'facility value' of questions (how easy or difficult they are) and the 'discrimination index' of questions (how well they separate the best candidates from the rest). Ideally, all questions should have been through trials with hundreds of students before using the questions in a formal exam. An advantage of multiple choice exams is that it is perfectly possible to arrange that students get not only their scores very quickly, but also detailed feedback reminding them of their correct decisions, and explaining why other decisions were incorrect.

2 **Make sure that candidates aren't going to be getting questions right for the wrong reasons.** Look for any giveaways in the keys or context of the questions.

3 **Watch out for cases where the best candidates choose a distractor.** This usually happens when they can see something wrong with the option which is supposed to be undeniably correct, or 'best'. This is best done manually, by scanning the responses from a large group of students, and with prior knowledge of who the most able students are.

4 **Start the exam with some relatively straightforward questions.** This helps anxious candidates to get into their stride, and is better than having such candidates thrown into a panic by an early tricky question.

5 **Help candidates to develop their skills at tackling multiple choice exams.** Give candidates past papers to practise on, and provide advice on the most effective techniques for tackling this form of exam.

6 **Get the timing right.** Decide whether you really want an against-the-clock exam. Find out how long candidates take on average. With a timed exam, there is some tendency for candidates to rush their decision making, and even if they have plenty of time left over, they are still left with a hangover legacy of questions where they made wrong decisions.

7 **Look for ways of making marking quick and easy.** When large numbers of candidates are involved, it is worth looking at optical mark-reading techniques or computer-aided testing formats.

8 **Get some colleagues to take your exam.** They may be surprised at things they find that they did not know, and they may give you some surprises too about what you thought were cut-and-dried questions.

9 **Form a regional network.** Teaming up with other colleagues in your discipline, who are also developing multiple choice testing, can help build up a good bank of tried and tested questions.

10 **Arrange for quick feedback to learners if possible.** If your exam is computer-generated, it can be designed to produce a score at any time, either when students have finished it, or as a running total. Students can also be given feedback on their choices either on-screen as they work through the test, or at the end as a printout.

Chapter 8 Assessing Independent Learning

One of the fundamental concerns about some traditional methods of assessment is that they fail to allow students to express the individuality of their achievement. Further concerns revolve around the fact that exam performance is in many respects an artificial skill, often seeming to encourage surface learning. We direct attention in this chapter to a range of alternative forms of assessment, which are closer to many of the skills students will need in their careers or postgraduate education.

In many vocational courses, students spend time on placement in companies or organisations. This is a crucial part of their educational experience, and we start this chapter with some suggestions about how we may go about designing appropriate assessment for work-based learning.

Developing research skills is crucial not only for students intending to go on to higher degrees, but also for those who may be seeking employment in research and development posts. Many courses in higher education include episodes of action research, and we make some suggestions about ways of trying to ensure that this is assessed appropriately.

We end this chapter with suggestions regarding the assessment of portfolios and reflective logs. Both of these formats allow students to assemble very individual pieces of evidence to bring forward for assessment, one giving a broad picture of the scope and diversity of their learning, and the other adding detail on self-evaluation and critical thinking.

39

Assessment and work-based learning

Many courses include a placement period, and the increasing use of accreditation of prior experiential learning in credit accumulation systems means that we need to look at ways of assessing material produced by students in work contexts, rather than just things students write up when back at college after their placements. In addition, work-based learning is often a crucial part of the work of part-time students. We have therefore not restricted our suggestions below to the assessment of work-based learning, but have given some tips on the planning of work-based learning in general. We hope that the following suggestions may help you tackle assessment of the diversity and variety of work-based learning.

1 **Involve employers, professional supervisors and colleagues.** They will need careful briefing, and negotiation may also be required to achieve their full cooperation, as they are often very busy people. Ways of involving them include asking them to produce testimonials, statements of competence, checklists and grids or simply to sign off students' own statements of competence or achievement.

2 **Give students some choice regarding placements.** Use a questionnaire to help find out which students want various kinds of placement. You may well not be able to satisfy everyone, but when possible, try to put students into the sort of organisation or firm that they most wish to experience.

3 **Allow students to arrange placements for themselves.** Some students will be able to do this, and it is worth giving them the chance to have increased ownership of their placement experience. Arranging their own placements allows such students to demonstrate additional organisational and interpersonal skills. Some students, however, will be less able to arrange their own placements (for example, overseas students who may not have sufficient knowledge about local possibilities), so it is important not to allow this factor to prejudice assessment.

4 **Be clear about the purpose of the assessment.** Is the assessment being done to satisfy a funding body, the university, or employers? Is the assessment primarily to aid students' learning? Or is the assessment primarily designed to help students develop skills and experience which will aid their future careers? Clarifying the purposes can help you decide the most appropriate forms of assessment.

5 **Get the balance right.** Work out carefully what proportion of students' overall assessment will be derived from their placements. Decide whether the related assessment should be on a pass/fail basis, or whether it should be attempted to classify it for degrees.

6 **Help students to keep their placements in perspective.** Students can become deeply involved in work done during placements, and there is the possibility that they may neglect some of the other things they should be doing, such as keeping their earlier learning consolidated ready for later exams.

7 **Expect placements to be very different.** If a group of students are spread through a number of companies or organisations, some will have a very good experience of placement, and others, through no fault of their own, can have an unsatisfactory experience. It is important that factors outside students' control are not allowed to prejudice assessment.

8 **Set up a meeting with previous students who have returned from placements.** Much valuable discussion can take place, and students about to go on placement can quiz a panel of those who have had their experience of it. The meeting may need planning well in advance to fit in with busy time schedules. Small group meetings are often more productive for such purposes.

9 **Consider carefully whether the mentor is well-placed to assess.** There can sometimes be complex confusions of role if the person who is the professional supporter or friend of the assessee is also the person who has to make critical evaluations for assessment purposes.

10 **Decide carefully whether to tutor-assess during workplace visits.** Visiting students on placement certainly gives tutors opportunities to gather data that may be relevant to assessment, but if assessment is on the agenda the whole nature of such visits changes.

11 **Use a learning contract.** These are particularly valuable for allowing students to demonstrate achievement within a changing environment, since they enable the renegotiation of outcomes when necessary. Using learning contracts also allows appropriate learning outcomes to be negotiated within the context of each placement.

12 **Include assessment of a work log.** Some professions prescribe the exact form such a log or work diary should take. In other work contexts it is possible for the course team or the students themselves to devise their own formats. It is often helpful if such logs include lists of learning outcomes, skills, or competences that students are expected to achieve and demonstrate, with opportunities to check these off and add comments as appropriate.

13 **Ask students to produce a reflective journal.** This can be a much more personal kind of document, and might include hopes, fears and feelings as well as more mundane accounts of actions and achievements. Assessing reflective journals can raise tricky issues of confidentiality and disclosure, but ways round such issues can be found, particularly if students are asked to submit for assessment edited extracts from their reflective journals.

14 **Consider using a portfolio.** A portfolio to demonstrate achievement at work can include suitably anonymised real products from the workplace (with the permission of the employer) as well as testimonials from clients, patients, support staff and others.

15 **Devise record keeping aids for students.** Providing students with skeleton portfolios or formats onto which to record reflective journals can help to make it easier for them to produce evidence in forms suitable for assessment, and makes assessing different students in different contexts easier. However, make sure that you don't inhibit students' freedom and creativity by providing too much structure.

16 **Use technology.** Students and tutors can communicate even more effectively on a regular basis now than ever before, through media such as e-mail, and the Internet. This makes it possible to supervise and support student learning anywhere in the world where the appropriate technology is available, and can be used most productively for interactive support from tutors and peers. Many institutions also make teaching materials available using technological media. This is particularly useful when access to traditional texts is difficult while students are on placement.

17 **Get students to set up tutorless support groups.** Where several students work for the same employer, they can often help each other's learning significantly, even if they are doing different courses or at different stages or levels of study. Employer cooperation is valuable here, particularly in providing rooms for meetings, and allowing staff release time.

18 **Encourage networking.** Students working at locations some distance apart can still collaborate actively, using e-mail, faxes, the phone, and ordinary post. Such collaboration can be particularly useful for day-release and part-time students, who often have little time in a packed working day at the university for group work or interaction.

19 **Use NVQ and GNVQ frameworks.** These have been established and calibrated and enable easy transition between the learning in the workplace and at the university. They already contain useful detail of the sorts of evidence that students may accumulate to demonstrate their achievement of particular competences.

20 **Don't lose the learning.** Consider asking students who have completed work placements to write their experiences up in the form of a journal article, perhaps for an in-house magazine or journal. A collection of these can help to disseminate their experiences. Joint articles written with employers are even more valuable, and help make links with employers better.

40

Assessing action research

Since action learning or action research is about improving students' professional experience through reflection and action, its assessment is both interesting and challenging. Importantly, action research has value in itself to the researcher, and therefore needs to be assessed with reference to the students' own workplace. There is no external reference for assessment of the value of action research other than the requirement that it strives to improve the quality of action within students' professional careers. The following ten questions point to the essence of action research, and provide the main criteria for its assessment.

1 **Does the research proposal identify a problem or issue clearly?** Does this directly link with the students' own professional practice?

2 **Is there evidence of a disciplined, systematic and critical approach to students' understanding of their practice?**

3 **Have the students reflected on their own beliefs and values?** Has this been shown to help them to understand the problems and issues under investigation in the research?

4 **Has the evidence collected by students been derived from investigations carried out within their workplace?** Is the evidence sufficiently specific, so that it is clear that it has not been collected from available sources elsewhere?

5 **Is there evidence of students involvement at a personal level in the research process?** It is worth checking that the individuality of students shows through in the processes they choose for their research, and the ways that they interpret and communicate their findings.

6 **Is the research directed towards improving the quality of the students' practice?** It is important to ensure that the research does not stray towards what has been readily researchable rather than what is directly relevant to the fields in which the students will practise.

7 **Has the search for new knowledge been determined by the nature of the improvements to practice sought by the students?** It is useful to examine how students have defined their aims and objectives for their research, and how relevant these are in terms of seeking pointers towards improved practice.

8 **Is there evidence of relating theory to improvements in students' practice?** Has appropriate theoretical underpinning been identified, and have concepts been integrated developmentally?

9 **Has the collection of evidence been largely the result of observation, discussion and reflection?** Is it subjective and qualitative rather than objective and quantitative?

10 **Has the research shed light on the possibilities for students' ongoing professional development?** Does this extend well beyond the immediate outcomes of the programme of action research undertaken?

41

Using learning contracts for assessment

Learning contracts enable students to negotiate how they will satisfy the assessment requirements of a course, either by devising their own learning outcomes, or by discussing what kinds of evidence they will need to assemble in order to satisfy specified learning outcomes in a more structured course. Learning contracts are useful in that they enable students to demonstrate individuality, gain credit for prior experience, and concentrate on what they can do rather than what they cannot do. The following tips can only provide a toe in the water for those who are considering using learning contracts (or are already doing so). Further reading is listed in the suggestions at the end of the book.

1 **Start by looking at the students' entry profiles.** This can be done by using a self-rating form to be completed by students, by discussion with tutors, or by other means of recognising prior achievement.

2 **Consider where the learning programme needs to lead.** Think about what final level of achievement is being targeted, and what kinds of evidence will be needed to demonstrate this.

3 **Plan for action.** Students and tutors will need to consider how students can progress towards the required learning outcomes, ideally expressing these processes in the form of action plans which include particular activities, deadlines, check points, and agreed means of collecting evidence.

4 **Evaluate achievement.** Students and tutors will need to monitor performance to see how the targets have been met from time to time. This will almost certainly be a cyclical process, with students going back to their original agreements for rethinking and replanning.

5 **Renegotiate.** Few learning contracts ever go completely to plan. They should be sufficiently flexible for students who have achieved more than they anticipated to incorporate this into the assignments, and to cope with the inevitable delays, pitfalls and disappointments that befall us all.

6 **Make your availability clear.** If effective monitoring of the learning agreements is to take place, there will need to be contact between tutors and students, and this should be fixed in advance. An 'open door' policy is not ideal, as under-confident students may well be perpetually knocking on your door, and the fiercely independent students may reject support because they don't realise when they need it.

7 **Stand back a bit.** Students learning independently need a different kind of support from those in traditional learning contexts. It is often difficult to balance the need to let students develop independently against our tendency as tutors to be directive and offer all the answers. Learning contracts are designed to let students take a more autonomous role in learning.

8 **Be supportive.** Students working on learning contracts will still need advice, for example, on where to look for appropriate reference sources, and they may well also need confidence building and reassurance. A light touch is usually best.

9 **Bring in a third party.** It is useful for students' progress, from devising their contracts to final evaluation, to be monitored by a mentor. The mentor need not be a member of staff, and could be a fellow student or friend chosen by the student. Some guidelines or training sessions for mentors are a useful aid.

10 **Publish a booklet of learning contracts that worked.** This helps your students formulate realistic learning contracts at appropriate levels. Preferably (with permission) include the names of the original students, who can then be tracked down by your present students for advice.

42

Assessing portfolios

Portfolios provide a valuable method of assessing what students have achieved, particularly in contexts outside the learning institution. They enable students to provide evidence of achievement of specified competences, sometimes as a result of a learning contract. These competences can be achieved from a variety of contexts including work, leisure and home and from independent study as well as the university itself. Portfolios provide students with plenty of opportunities for self-expression but if students are not given guidance on the range, volume and form of presentation of materials, the portfolios can become unwieldly and difficult and time-consuming to assess. The following suggestions should help you minimise these risks, and help your students get the most from portfolios.

1 **Quality not quantity counts.** Students should be advised not to submit every piece of paper they have collected over the learning period, otherwise the volume of material can be immense.

2 **Get students to provide route maps.** Portfolios are easier to assess if the material is carefully structured, and accompanied by a reflective account which not only outlines the contents but also asserts which of the criteria each piece of evidence contributes towards.

3 **Get students to provide a structure.** Portfolio elements should be clearly labelled and numbered for easy reference. If loose leaf folders are used, dividers should be labelled to enable easy access to material. All supplementary material such as audiotapes, videos, drawings, computer programs, tables, graphs, and so on should be appropriately marked and cross-referenced.

4 **Be clear about what you are assessing.** While detailed mark schemes are not really appropriate for portfolios, it is still necessary to have clear and explicit criteria, both for the students' use and to guide assessment.

5 **Structure your feedback.** Students may well have spent many hours assembling portfolios and may have a great deal of personal investment in them. To give their work number marks only (or pass/fail) may seem small reward. Consider using an assessment form so that your notes and comments can be directly relayed to the students, particularly in cases where required elements are incomplete or missing.

6 **Encourage creativity.** For some students, this may be the first time they have been given an opportunity to present their strengths in a different way. Hold a brainstorming session about the possible contents of portfolios, for example, which may include videos, recorded interviews, newspaper articles, and so on.

7 **Provide opportunities for self-assessment.** Having completed their portfolios, a valuable learning experience in itself is to let the students assess them. A short exercise is to ask them: 'In the light of your experience of producing a portfolio, what do you consider you did especially well, and what would you now do differently?'

8 **Assess in a team.** If possible set aside a day as a team. Write your comments about each portfolio, and then pass them round for others to add to. In this way, learners get feedback that is more comprehensive, and assessors get to see a more diverse range of portfolios.

9 **Set up an exhibition.** Portfolios take a long time to complete and assess. By displaying them (with students' permission) their valuable experience can be shared.

10 **Think about where and when you will mark portfolios.** They are not nearly as portable as scripts, and you may need equipment such as video or audio playback facilities to review evidence. It may be helpful therefore to set aside time when you can book a quiet, well-equipped room where you are able to spread out materials and look at a number of portfolios together. This will help you get an overview, and makes it easier to get a feel for standards.

43

Assessing reflective logs

Reflective logs, by their very nature, are made in different ways by different students. Where it is intended to assess such work, it is useful to specify the format and structures within which candidates can demonstrate their reflections. The following suggestions may help you to formulate such a framework.

1 **Set the brief clearly in advance.** It is easier to mark reflective logs if students have a clear idea of what they are trying to achieve. This will avoid you having to plough through endless ramblings which are irrelevant to the assessment task.

2 **Identify clearly what evidence will demonstrate achievement of the assessment criteria.** Ensure that the criteria used are measurable. It is difficult, for example, to assess whether a piece of writing represents 'an honest personal account' when all that is available is the candidate's work, without a framework against which to judge it.

3 **Quantify the amount of evidence required.** For example, specify 'three examples of…' or 'illustrations of applying four methods to…'. This makes it much simpler to give fair assessments to a range of different candidates, each approaching the task of producing reflective logs in their own ways.

4 **Consider whether it is necessary to grade or give marks.** Conscientious engagement with the task may be all that you need to see evidence of. This may be sufficient for a pass/fail assessment outcome. If some kind of grade is required, it may be best to go for a system of banding (for example, fail, pass, merit, distinction), but where this is the case, it will be essential to provide students (and fellow-assessors) with an assessment protocol to give guidance on what exactly would constitute the kind of performance necessary for each level of achievement.

5 **Consider permitting the submission of extracts for assessment, rather than the whole reflective log.** Some areas of work may lead students to write personal or confidential matters into what becomes a really meaningful reflective journal. They may not wish to reveal these areas to their assessors, moderators and external examiners.

6 **Give candidates reflective logs to assess, and ask them to formulate assessment criteria.** This helps them to identify good practice to apply to their own future reflective logs.

7 **Give students the chance to develop their skills.** It is best to introduce reflective logs early in a course, so that students have time to acquire the appropriate skills.

8 **Start small.** Build up confidence gradually. Even a very short reflective exercise can be extremely valuable, especially when students get plenty of feedback on it. It is easier to give a lot of feedback on a short exercise!

9 **If time allows, skim-read the whole reflective log first.** Then read more closely, looking for evidence of the criteria being achieved.

10 **Consider letting groups of students make reflective logs.** Students can generate greater levels of reflection when bouncing ideas off each other, and discussing matters arising.

Chapter 9 Self, Peer And Group Assessment

We strongly believe in the power of student self-assessment and peer-assessment, and in the importance of using assessed student groupwork. We have postponed much of our discussion of these aspects of assessment till towards the end of this book because we suggest that all of these processes of assessment can be extended to most of the formats of assessment that we have already addressed.

Students learn a great deal from each other, and with larger student numbers, the importance of peer feedback increases as the availability of tutor feedback decreases. Setting up and facilitating student peer-assessment can provide students with deep learning experiences as well as with a wealth of feedback to evaluate.

It can be argued that a measure of success of an education system should be that students should not actually need anyone to assess their knowledge or performance, but that they should be able to do it for themselves. We provide suggestions for implementing student self-assessment, and for equipping students for the rest of their careers with well-developed self-evaluation and self-appraisal skills.

We continue this chapter with some suggestions about setting up and assessing student groupwork. The skills involved in successful collaboration and cooperation are every bit as valuable as those involved in independent work, and are much valued by employers and managers. We believe that using assessed groupwork provides a sound basis for helping students to develop these important skills.

We end this chapter with suggestions about assessing open learners. There are many reasons why assessment needs to be handled particularly carefully in open learning, not least of which is the fact that open learners (especially on distance education programmes) are often quite isolated, and lack the peer support experienced by college-based learners.

44

Conditions where peer-assessment works well

Peer-assessment can be an invaluable means of involving students closely in their own and each other's learning. It is not a 'quick fix' solution to reduce staff marking time, as it is intensive in its use of tutor time at the briefing and development stages. It has high pay-off in terms of improved learning. The following suggestions show some areas where peer-assessment produces excellent benefits.

1 **Student presentations.** Peer-assessment is particularly useful for the style and process of student presentations. It can also be useful for the content side of presentations, when the topics are sufficiently shared so that students are well-informed enough to make judgements on the content of each other's presentations.

2 **Reports.** Peer-assessment helps to alert learners to good and bad practice in report-writing, and helps them develop awareness of the importance of structure, coherence and layout in reports.

3 **Essay plans.** Peer-assessment of essay plans can widen learners' horizons about different ways of brainstorming the content and structure of essays. It takes almost as much creative thinking to design the content of an essay plan as it would to produce the final essay, so peer-assessing such plans helps students to share a lot of ideas in a relatively short time.

4 **Calculations.** Peer-assessing correct answers is simple and quick. Peer-assessment allows students to identify exactly where things went wrong when marking incorrect answers, and alerts learners to potential trouble spots to avoid in the future.

5 **Interviews.** Peer-assessment allows students to exchange a range of opinions, attitudes and reactions to each other's interview performance, in a less threatening way than can be the case when such performance is tutor-assessed.

6 **Annotated bibliographies.** Peer-assessment of bibliographies can be a fast and effective way of alerting learners to *other* sources of reference, which learners working on their own might otherwise have overlooked.

7 **Practical work.** Peer-assessment of experimental work can allow learners to receive feedback on their practical skills, when tutor-assessment of such skills may be threatening – or not possible, for example, due to limited tutor availability when large groups of students are involved.

8 **Poster displays.** Peer-assessment of poster displays can be a rapid way of alerting learners to a wide range of approaches to the visual presentation of ideas.

9 **Portfolios.** Where students are familiar with all the requirements for the successful demonstration of their achievements through portfolios, they are often highly competent in assessing each other's, particularly if they themselves have recently undertaken a similar task.

10 **Exhibitions and artefacts.** Art students in particular have a long tradition of participating in critiques of each other's paintings, plans, models, garments, sculptures and so on. Students participating in 'crits' learn a lot about the level of work required, and the ways in which aesthetic judgments of work are formed within their own particular subject.

45

Starting to use peer-assessment

Increasingly, peer-assessment is being used to involve students more closely in their learning and its evaluation, and to help to enable students really understand what is required of them. It can have enormous benefits in terms of learning gain, but is not to be regarded as a short-cut to tutors wishing to lighten their assessment burden. Setting up peer-assessment may well involve greater effort from tutors in the early stages, although long term there will be savings in tutor time. The following suggestions may help you get started with student peer-assessment.

1 **Take it a bit at a time.** Some people (students and tutors) find the use of peer-assessment very radical, so it is a good idea to introduce it gradually, on a small scale, until you, your colleagues and students are confident about how it will work best.

2 **Keep everyone in the picture.** Tell everyone what you are doing and why. Students and colleagues need to understand the thinking behind what you are doing, to avoid them perceiving it as a soft option or abdication of responsibility. If they understand that peer-assessment is actually part of the learning process, they may find it more acceptable.

3 **Provide mark-free rehearsal opportunities.** This helps students get the hang of what is required of them, and also builds in an opportunity for students to get interim feedback at a stage when there is time to bring about improvements.

4 **Provide, or negotiate, really clear assessment criteria.** Students should not be able to over-mark friends or penalise enemies if the criteria are unambiguous and explicit. All marks should be justifiable by reference to the criteria, and to the evidence of achievement of them.

5 **Make peer-assessment marks meaningful.** Some argue that peer review is really only suitable for feedback purposes. However, if students are to take peer-assessment seriously, it should count for something, even if it is only a small proportion of the final grade. You may prefer to 'parallel mark', with tutor grades counting as well as averaged peer grades if this is appropriate.

6 **Moderate peer-assessment.** To ensure that the students see peer-assessment as fair, tutors must overview the marks awarded and provide a 'court of appeal' if students feel justice has not been done. This may mean offering vivas to any dissatisfied candidates.

7 **Keep the system simple.** Try not to give yourself really complicated addition and averaging tasks to do after peer-assessment has taken place. Too many separate components make it laborious to arrive at final marks. If the numerical side can't be simplified, it is worth using computer programs to do the donkey work!

8 **Involve students in the assessment criteria.** You can do this by involving students in the generation of assessment criteria, and in the weighting given to each criterion. Alternatively, you can provide the criteria in the first instance, and give students lots of opportunities to ask questions about what they really mean.

9 **Allow plenty of time.** Just because you can assess a poster display or an essay fairly quickly doesn't mean that students will be able to do so too, especially if groups are assessing other groups and are required to provide a mark by consensus. Presentations always over-run, and students will tend to make snap conclusions and 'guesstimates' when under pressure regarding time.

10 **Monitor student achievement.** It's a good idea to review how well students are peer-assessing, by the same kinds of methods you may use to review your own assessment, to ensure reliability and validity of marking. It is often reassuring for students (and colleagues) to see that peer-assessment using explicit criteria, and based on the production of clearly specified evidence, produces data that are very similar to marks produced by tutors themselves.

46

Starting to use self-assessment

There are many levels on which student self-assessment may be used, ranging from activities intended simply to promote reflective learning, to formal strategies which allow student self-assessment to count in their overall marks. If we can help our students to develop self-evaluative skills, so that they are accurately able to judge the effectiveness of their own performances, we will equip them with the kinds of skills that will help them to learn throughout their lives. This should ensure they achieve better performance at university, and are more sought after by employers. The following suggestions may help you decide when to introduce elements of student self-assessment into your courses.

1 **Make self-assessment an integral element of learning.** Help students to become lifelong learners who can evaluate their own performance after they have finished formal study. This is a valuable skill which will help them in their professional careers.

2 **Think of some things that no-one but students can really assess.** For example, students alone can give a rating to how much effort they put into a task, how strong their motivation is in a particular subject, or how much they believe they have improved something over a period of time.

3 **Give students practice at positively evaluating themselves.** For example, give them nine post-its and ask them to list nine qualities or skills they have, and get them to prioritise them in a ranking order one to nine.

4 **Emphasise the crucial relationship between criteria, evidence and self-evaluation.** Help students to learn to make balanced judgments about themselves that relate directly to the assessment criteria, by providing clear evidence of what has been achieved.

5 **Encourage the use of reflective accounts and journals, to promote self-evaluation.** By encouraging students to review their own performance regularly through journaling, they can build up a picture of their own work over a period of time.

6 **Support students in self-assessment.** Give them lots of guidance at the outset, then progressively let them take a greater degree of responsibility for their assessment as their understanding of the process matures.

7 **Help students to get to grips with assessment criteria.** Let them discuss what the criteria will mean in practice, and get them to describe exactly what sorts of performance or evidence will demonstrate achievement of the criteria.

8 **Help students to prepare for self-assessment by assessing peers.** It is often easier to make judgments about their own work when they have participated in looking critically at what others have done.

9 **Include self-assessment when assessing group process.** Frequently students are asked to peer-assess each other's contribution to group tasks. It is also feasible for them to assess realistically what they have added themselves to the process, applying the same notions of criteria and evidence as they did to their peers.

10 **Use open learning materials.** Most such materials include a lot of self-assessment exercises in one way or another. Usually, the primary benefit of these is not strictly self-assessment, but the use of feedback to students who have had a try at the exercises.

11 **Provide computer-based self-assessment opportunities for students.** It can help students to find out a lot about how their learning is going when computer-based packages are available in a library or resource room, where they can check their knowledge in the comfort of privacy. Such packages can also provide feedback and direction, as well as giving students a quantitative indication of the state of their learning.

12 **Provide self-assessment opportunities as diagnostic aids.** Open learning or computer-based packages can include sets of questions designed to help students identify which sections of their work may need particular attention. The packages can also include remedial 'loops' which students experiencing particular difficulties can be routed through.

13 **Use self-assessment to establish existing competence.** Self-assessment exercises and tests can be a quick way of enabling students to establish how much of their prior learning is relevant to the prerequisite knowledge for their next course or module. This can help students avoid wasting time studying things they have already covered sufficiently.

14 **Use self-assessment sometimes in lectures and tutorials.** For example, when students have brought along coursework expecting to hand it in for tutor-marking, it can be useful to lead the whole group through self-assessment against clear marking guidelines. The work can still be handed in, and it is usually much faster and easier to moderate students' own assessments than to mark the work from scratch.

15 **Use self-assessment as part of learning contracts.** The act of self-assessing is a very useful one for students. When they are producing evidence specifically relating to their own learning contracts, it can be useful to ask them to self-assess how well they have demonstrated their achievement of some of their intended outcomes. One way of firming this up is to allocate some tutor-assessed marks for the quality of their own self-assessment; this also allows students to be given feedback on this.

16 **Suggest that students use video to self-assess their presentation skills informally.** Watching videotapes in the comfort of privacy can allow students to reflect very deeply on their skills. In fact, it is sometimes useful to suggest that students view each other's videos informally after self-assessing, to put the self-critical evaluations some students may have made of themselves into more comfortable perspective.

17 **Include self-assessment with student portfolios.** Ask students to include in their portfolios self-evaluations of their work. Reserve some of the marks for portfolios for the quality and depth of students' self-appraisal.

18 **Experiment with non-print media for self-assessment.** For example, when art students are preparing an exhibition or display, ask them to provide an interim self-critique on audiotape.

19 **Make the last part of an exam a section of self-evaluation.** Ask students to use this to reflect on their performance in the exam, and the factors that helped and hindered their achievement.

20 **Get students to self-assess added value.** Getting students to self-appraise the added value that a course or module had given them can be a useful adjunct to student feedback procedures, and helps students to put their learning into perspective in the overall context of their development.

47

Self and peer marking

This is the most basic way of involving students in their own, and each other's, assessment. Usually it does not involve a high level of evaluation, since it often relies on correct or model answers provided by tutors. However it can be used to provide additional feedback opportunities for students, particularly when the assessments are not part of the overall summative assessment process.

1 **Don't give the solutions out too early.** Get students in pairs or in groups to look at their own and each other's work, and discuss among themselves what they think is right or wrong with it. Only then let them see the solutions you have provided, by which stage much learning will have taken place in the dialogue.

2 **Provide 'surgery' opportunities.** Students may well wish to interrogate your 'correct' answers. Check up on any 'almost right' solutions, and take the chance to participate in 'yes, but...' discussions. These sessions also provide chances for learning to take place.

3 **Make sure that the students can't get their hands on the answers before they have attempted the tasks.** When the answers are too easily available, it tends to demotivate students from making real attempts at finding solutions for themselves. Of course, in some contexts, such as when using open learning materials, it may not always be possible to control the availability of answers. Then, it's worth appealing to students' better nature, saying 'you can of course cheat, but it won't help you very much in the long run'.

4 **Give students the chance to find out why they were right, as well as why they were wrong.** This multiplies the ways in which students can benefit from self- and peer-marking.

5 **Use self- or peer-marking as a rehearsal opportunity for summative assessment.** Let the students see what is expected of them, by giving them a practice assessment task (such as assessing answers to last year's exam papers). Let students mark themselves against the tutor-provided marking guide. This can enhance very effectively their performance in the final assessment.

6 **Use computer-based assessment.** Some students who like computers will often take avidly to self-assessment tasks on-screen, when they would shy away from group activities. Do not underestimate the learning and reinforcement that can take place using multiple choice questions on-screen, particularly when feedback responses are provided in the package.

7 **Let one group of students help you to develop model answers for the next.** Suitably anonymised extracts of excellent examples from the first run of an assignment can be used (with student permission) to provide varied and appropriate models against which students can measure their own achievement. (This, after all, is a process that happens informally in many cases.)

8 **Let students practise making 'standards' decisions on examples of past students' work.** Alternatively, specially composed 'examples' can be prepared for this. Ask students in groups to assign 'Pass, Merit or Distinction' to some examples of work. Ask each group to write a short statement defending why each decision was reached.

9 **Allow student self-assessment before tutor assessment sometimes.** Produce a brief sheet for students to fill in just before handing in some work to be tutor-marked. Ask, for example, what mark or grade they believe their work deserves, what improvements they would attempt to make if doing it again, and what they think is the best aspect of the work they are submitting.

10 **Sometimes, return tutor-marked work with feedback comments, but no marks or grades.** Write down your own mark or grade in your own records. Ask students to self-assess their work in the light of your feedback comments, and hand it in again a week later with their own marks or grades on it. Expect nine out of ten students to more-or-less agree with you! Write on your own marks at this point, and arrange one-to-one discussions with the few students where there is a significant difference between their self-assessment and your own judgement.

48

Assessing groups

The ability to work as an effective member of a team is a key skill required in most careers. The development of this skill can be encouraged by including student groupwork in courses. When facilitated effectively and assessed sensitively, student groupwork can be most productive and can also be fun.

1 **Set the scene appropriately.** Help students to understand how beneficial group work can be to them. Share your thinking with colleagues as well as students. It is important that everyone is aware how the student groupwork is to be assessed. Assessing such work without any explanation can be a devastating experience for the students assessed.

2 **Introduce assessed groupwork early.** Don't wait until the final year of a course. This is partly because students may have become fixed in their expectations regarding assessment, and also because in many courses much depends on students' final year performance, and it would be unfair to change the assessment practices at this late stage. When groupwork assessment is introduced early in a course, students are more likely to see it as natural and non-threatening.

3 **Don't allocate marks early on.** Too much detail about marks can detract from the main purpose of using groupwork assessment – that of developing students' skills at working together. Before setting assessed groupwork tasks, introduce a few exercises to help students develop and reflect on group skills.

4 **Use exercises such as 'building a paper tower' to develop a team spirit.** Give each group six sheets of paper, scissors, and Sellotape, and ask them to build the tallest free-standing tower. Don't allow cheating! Then get the students to discuss how their groups worked together. Allocating a non-participating observer to each group can be useful.

5 **Introduce assessment criteria slowly.** Set an activity for the students and give them some of the criteria. Ask them to add two further criteria of their own, and to decide how many marks should be allocated to each criterion.

6 **Allow time for debriefing.** The most important part of the learning pay-off is when students analyse their successes, and some of the 'could have done better by...' aspects of their activities in the group.

7 **Be clear about what you are trying to assess.** Work out whether you are assessing the product or outcome of the groupwork, or whether it is the processes that are being measured. Processes and product can be quite different, and require different approaches to assessment. In some group activities only products may lend themselves to assessment, while in other activities it may be only processes.

8 **Let students choose their own criteria.** This is best done after students have already had some experience of groupwork. Each group could be briefed to do the same activity, but asked to devise its own set of criteria, using which other groups will mark them. This is usually a very positive learning experience, leading to greater awareness among students of the importance of the clarity of assessment criteria.

9 **Be aware of dangers associated with assessing individuals in a group.** This can lead to great traumas and heated debates. If individual contributions are to be assessed it is very important that the criteria are known, discussed, and agreed at the outset. It is usually better to assess such contributions after the team has developed confidence and trust. (See Brown, Rust and Gibbs, 1994, for six methods of group assessment suitable for different contexts.)

10 **Consider the ways that groups can be formed.** Do you wish students to choose their own groups? (Students tend to self-select by ability, with able students strategically choosing each other, leaving the less-able to make up their own teams later.) Do you want to allocate students randomly, to provide an element of fairness? (This works well on small scale projects where the teams can be rotated.) Or do you want to put students into learning teams, where you select groups to ensure a balance of the mixture of experience, ability and skills? This is particularly useful in providing a productive cooperative learning experience, but takes a higher level of organisational skill for you to arrange it.

49

Assessing open learners

In many ways, good assessment practice for open learning overlaps with many of our suggestions throughout this book – particularly regarding the provision of feedback. However, such feedback needs to be articulated even more carefully for open learners than for conventional students. We have listed twenty suggestions regarding the task of tutoring open learners effectively.

1 **Get to know your open learners.** Sometimes, in distance education, tutors and learners may never actually meet. Even then, exchanges of correspondence can open up good communication, and this is best done well before the more formal role of assessing comes in.

2 **Make the first assignment a dry run.** It can take much of the pressure off learners, if they know that the first tutor-marked assignment is essentially a 'setting the parameters' exercise.

3 **Remember how distance learners may feel about sending in their first assignments for assessment.** For many, it may be the first time for years they've submitted written work to a tutor for assessment. They can be anxious, excited, vulnerable and fearful about the prospect of someone assessing their work.

4 **Remember how important feedback is.** Feedback from tutors is all the more crucial for open and distance learners. Your comments on written assignments may be the main way (or the only way) that such learners receive feedback from an expert. Ticks and crosses are not nearly enough.

5 **Mind your language.** Remember that simple words such as 'but', 'however' and 'although' are usually followed by bad news of one kind or another, and can cause learners' feelings to sink. Learners can't see the reassuring smile on your face or the twinkle in your eye when they've only got your words to look at.

6 **Be careful not to demotivate completely!** Try to avoid completely using words such as 'failed', 'have not grasped', 'misunderstood', or even 'adequate' or 'satisfactory'. Such words can come across very negatively to learners who are taking every word you write seriously.

7 **Use assignment return sheets or letters for your main comments.** It's important that open learners don't get their work back covered with your comments between the lines. Give yourself space to explain things clearly and legibly.

8 **Keep a copy of your substantive comments.** It's all too easy to forget exactly what you've said to each learner when you're returning their marked work to them. A copy of your assignment return sheet or letter can be really helpful to you when you may need to follow up some issues in, for example, telephone discussions with learners or subsequent assignments.

9 **Try to return marked work as quickly as possible.** Open learners get much more value from your feedback if they get your comments while they can still remember the detail of the thinking they put into their assignments.

10 **Invite open learners to tell you more about what they want from your feedback.** Some may specifically ask you for comments on their style or grammar. Some may want particular comments about whether they were successful in tackling areas they found difficult.

11 **Consider preparing model answers or discussion notes to return to learners with their marked work.** This can save you having to repeat the same comments over and over again to different open learners, and can be very useful to learners in helping them see the standards you're expecting of them.

12 **Be particularly clear about the wording of assignment questions.** When working with open learners, it is often sensible to redraft assignments on the basis of your experience of marking the first batch from learners.

13 **Save examples of good assignments.** With their owners' permission, it can be helpful to be able to send good examples to learners who had particular problems with an assignment.

14 **If you're marking alongside other tutors, take particular care with inter-tutor reliability.** It's useful to check that your feedback and standards are similar to those of other tutors marking the same assignments.

15 **Ask your learners regularly how they're finding your marking.** It's useful to know whether they are getting what they need from your comments and explanations, and they will often surprise you about areas where you thought you had made yourself quite clear!

16   **Consider being an open learner yourself.** It can be very valuable to subject yourself to the experience of having your work marked by someone else! Most tutors who experience this find that it affects the way they communicate with open learners.

17   **Keep good records.** If you're dealing with learners who may telephone you, or who may meet you face-to-face from time to time, it's important for you to be able to tune in rapidly to where each individual is in their work.

18   **Ask open learners to set you questions.** Some learners will do this anyway, but it is worth encouraging the rest to write down in the form of questions anything that they are having difficulty with in their studies. This will of course increase your workload, but it can pay off in terms of your learners' success in their studies.

19   **Don't be over-defensive regarding the learning materials.** Often, learners' questions and problems will reveal deficiencies in the learning materials, and it can often pay you to write a 'replacement page 25' to overcome a particular problem that several learners have alerted you to.

20   **Give study-skills advice.** Open learners often miss out on the informal tips tutors pass on in face-to-face sessions with students. Open learners may welcome particularly advice about revision strategies and exam technique.

Chapter 10 Assessing Competence And Transferable Skills

Our final chapter looks at some of the factors involved in developing and assessing students' competences and transferable skills.

Once it was common to write a syllabus simply as a list of the principal topics to be covered by students. Now, we are expected to provide much more detail. Increasingly syllabus content is being expressed in terms of the intended learning outcomes to be achieved by students. The National Council for Vocational Qualifications uses the definitions 'elements of competence', 'performance criteria', 'evidence descriptors' and 'range statements'. Many people find this interlinked terminology confusing. We hope that the sections in this chapter will help you to unravel the jargon and design a successful competence-based assessment framework.

50

Writing elements of competence

The next few sets of suggestions are strongly linked. In practice, it is not sensible to identify elements of competence in full detail, then to go on to specify performance criteria, evidence descriptors and range statements. It is better to be drafting them all in parallel. We've arranged our suggestions under each heading with this in mind.

1 **Look at some examples already written.** Many education and training programmes are already expressed, with varying levels of success (!), in competence terminology. For example, General National Vocational Qualifications in England and Wales use such systems, as do various management development programmes. Much can be learned about how to go about designing competence frameworks (and about how *not* to!), by looking carefully at a range of existing examples.

2 **Express prerequisite competences.** Most courses or modules don't start from scratch. It is normal to express the skills and knowledge which students starting a course are reasonably expected to have developed already. However, it may not be precise enough just to refer to earlier studies they have done by course title or subject. It is better to pin down some of the principal aspects of competence and knowledge that students should have derived from these earlier courses, which will be needed as starting points for their development in the new course.

3 **Move beyond your subject, towards what students will be able to *do* after they have studied it.** Some of the skills and competences which students will develop will depend on subject-specific expertise they develop. However, there is also likely to be a range of general skills which students will develop alongside their subject-specific ones.

4 **Think in terms of intended learning outcomes.** Look at what students should be expected to become able to do when they have successfully completed each stage of their learning. Phrase statements of learning outcomes in terms of things that students 'can do' as draft elements of competence.

5 **Check that elements of competence relate to things that *all* successful students will be able to demonstrate.** These should be achievable targets for all students, not just goals for the most successful ones. The *level* to which students will demonstrate each element of competence is dealt with in the finer detail of a competence framework.

6 **Make use of syllabus aims and objectives, if already formulated.** In syllabus specifications for the Business and Technology Education Council (BTEC) in England and Wales, for example, the intended learning outcomes may well already be expressed in terms of the actions that students will be able to perform after learning each topic. It is normally a relatively simple editing task to adjust such objectives to turn them into learning outcomes in 'can do' competence language.

7 **Don't forget values and ethics.** A major criticism of many existing competence frameworks is that they are entirely based on evidence which may or may not be underpinned with values. Don't be afraid to add competences requiring students to show evidence of upholding sensibly chosen values.

8 **Avoid expressing competences in terms of knowledge or understanding.** Although it may well be essential that students develop such knowledge and understanding, try to express elements of competence in terms of the things that students will be able to do to *demonstrate* these qualities.

9 **Beware of trivial competences.** In some contexts, there is the risk of stating the obvious when expressing competences. The obvious may still need to be stated, but it is best to do so in such a way that it is clear that the competences concerned relate to appropriate levels of student development.

10 **Think ahead to the assessment.** When identifying elements of competence remember that these are to form the foundation for measuring student achievement. Be careful not to write magnificent looking outcomes which could not possibly be measured objectively.

11 **Consult the market.** When designing a new competence framework relevant to students following particular employment directions, it is very useful to bring in employers early in the design stage, and help them to tell you exactly what sorts of things they want their future employees to be able to do.

12 **Postpone going into too much detail too early.** Elements of competence are only the first step in defining and expressing measurable competences. In most cases, the elements should remain broad and simple, with subsequent elaboration to be achieved by defining 'performance criteria, evidence descriptors and range statements'.

13 **Decide whether you need 'core' competences and optional ones.** Sometimes it can be too narrow to restrict the agenda to things all students should do. Under such circumstances it can be useful to specify a number of optional competences, and maybe add an indication of how many of these, out of the total, students should achieve.

51

Working out performance criteria

As we indicated in the previous set of suggestions, it is best that all aspects of a competence framework are developed together. Here, we have tried to identify the particular factors to be thought about in the context of spelling out performance criteria.

1 **Turn each element of competence into several specific actions that successful students will become able to perform.** Look at the sorts of things they will be expected to do in their professional work after leaving university, but be careful to specify the performance criteria in terms of actions they will actually have the opportunity to perform in the context of their studies.

2 **Make sure that each performance criterion is demonstrable.** Don't include things that students may well be *able* to demonstrate, if there would not be any possibility of actually giving them the chance to demonstrate them during the course.

3 **Expect each element of competence to require several performance criteria to cover it.** Most competences have a number of facets. It is normal for an element of competence to take between six and twelve performance criteria to cover it in a rounded way. If you end up with more than these, you may need to consider whether the element of competence concerned needs further subdividing.

4 **Think about hybrid performance criteria.** Often, there will be performance criteria which link to several elements of competence rather than to a single element. It is important that performance criteria are not stultified by trying to tie these broader ones to single elements of competence.

5 **Think ahead to the conditions under which the performance criteria will be demonstrated.** These can include whether students will be working alone or with other people, and whether they will have access to information and data. It can often become longwinded and clumsy to express these separately alongside each performance criterion, and the detail may need to be reserved for inclusion in evidence descriptors or range statements, but it is important to have this detail in mind while phrasing the performance criteria.

6 **Think ahead to the different levels to which each performance criterion can be shown to have been achieved.** These details will be relevant to the formulation of assessment criteria differentiating (for example) between pass, merit and distinction grades, or between successive classes of degree performance. It is best, however, to keep the performance criteria general and simple, and reserve the information about levels for inclusion in evidence descriptors and range statements.

7 **Think ahead to the nature of the evidence against which the performance criteria will be assessed.** In due course, specification of this evidence will play a vital part in the assessment scheme for the demonstration of the competences. When it is not easy to be clear about the forms that evidence may take, it is usually best to make adjustments to the performance criteria.

8 **Look for gaps.** Ask yourself, and other people, 'are there *other* things that any successful student should be able to show that they can do?' If necessary, revisit the elements of competence, adding new ones to cover any important aspects that may not be there already.

9 **Look beyond the subject.** It is normal for some performance criteria to relate to personal or transferable skills. Don't assume that these will have been covered in some other module. It is best to make performance criteria comprehensive enough to address everything that is relevant to each element of competence in the context of the course or module.

10 **Don't be too ambitious.** Remember that performance criteria are going to be the basis for assessment. Every important performance criterion should be associated with some kind of assessment, otherwise students can't be credited with having demonstrated the elements of competence concerned.

52

Writing evidence descriptors

In competence frameworks, student performance is judged not on the basis of what they know, but on what they can show. It is therefore important to be clear about the nature, range and standard of evidence we require students to produce. The following suggestions should help you strike an appropriate balance between evidence and achievement.

1 **Decide on 'mandatory' evidence.** This should cover minimum levels of achievement which will be considered to be adequate proof that performance criteria have been met sufficiently for the elements of competence associated with them to have been achieved.

2 **Include varied forms of evidence.** It is important, for example, that students are not measured all the time on the basis of similar forms of evidence, such as written reports. Some students are better at producing one form of evidence than another, and we need to try to ensure that such students are not disadvantaged.

3 **Work out an agenda of alternative possibilities for evidence.** When you intend students to use their initiative and creativity regarding the nature of the evidence with which they demonstrate their achievement of a performance criterion, give examples to help them select and collect evidence.

4 **Allow for students who wish to do it their way.** Arrange for students to have the opportunity to negotiate with you alternative forms of evidence they can assemble to demonstrate their achievement of performance criteria.

5 **Accept appropriate evidence from the past.** There is little point requiring students to re-invent the wheel. Make it possible for them to bring forward evidence of other work they have already done, which links directly to performance criteria in your competence framework.

6 **Be sensible about overlaps with other subjects.** In competence frameworks, there is the possibility that several performance criteria will be similar in different modules. Where possible, it is desirable to make the evidence descriptors sufficiently unique to each module, so that students completing one module can't claim that they have also achieved most of the performance criteria relating to another.

7 **Make sure that not too much evidence is required.** There is a tendency for students (and staff!) to collect too much evidence relating to a given performance criterion, when they should be aiming to collect a more diverse collection of evidence, spanning several performance criteria. It is worth specifying the intended quantities of evidence as 'rules of thumb', either in the evidence descriptors or in range statements, setting the parameters underpinning the collection and presentation of evidence.

8 **Develop evidence descriptors in terms of standards.** Having established evidence descriptors for the successful demonstration of performance criteria, it is possible to give details of the additional evidence quality which will relate to higher levels of competence, for example, 'merit' or 'distinction' rather than 'pass'. A similar approach can be used where Degree work is assessed using a competence approach, by specifying evidence descriptors relating to the hierarchy of pass, 2:2, 2:1 and 1st.

9 **Look again at the evidence descriptors and decide what has been missed!** It's often possible to say 'anyone demonstrating competence X *must* somewhere have done such-and-such' only to discover that the appropriate evidence has still not been specified anywhere in the competence framework. It is usually necessary to go back in such cases and add further performance criteria relating to such evidence.

10 **Keep the evidence descriptors as understandable as possible.** Keep the language simple and straightforward. One of the problems of competence-based approaches is the tendency for curriculum developers to get wrapped up in jargon and convoluted expressions, which often mean nothing to the students themselves.

53

Writing range statements

In this final set of suggestions regarding competence frameworks, we present a few ideas about the role of range statements. We conclude with some overall suggestions pertaining to the whole framework.

1 **Use range statements to complete the competence framework.** The combination of elements of competence, performance criteria, and evidence descriptors should be made completely self-explanatory by the additional detail provided in range statements. These should alert students to any additional specifications regarding the nature, quality, quantity and standards of the evidence they should provide for each element of competence.

2 **Use range statements as illustrations.** Include examples of things that will provide satisfactory evidence of the achievement of the learning outcomes. These can be particularly useful to students if they are framed in a straightforward way, and relate to real life practice.

3 **Provide guidelines rather than imperatives.** While it is useful to be specific, it is important to clarify that original, divergent and creative responses from students are also possible and credit-worthy.

4 **Use range statements to address collaborative working.** While it may be necessary for students to provide evidence that demonstrates individual achievement, it is also important that they have the opportunity to display the cooperative aspects of their work.

Some unifying points about competence frameworks...

5 **It's best to number everything!** Assign number systems to elements of competence, performance criteria, evidence descriptors and range statements, so you can refer students easily to particular components in the framework.

6 **Cross-reference everything.** For example, indicate clearly which perform-ance indicators are to be demonstrated by each specified piece of evidence. Link evidence to the relevant elements of competence.

7 **Decide where grading is appropriate and possible.** Not all competences, performance criteria, or pieces of evidence can be graded. Some can only be used on a pass-or-fail basis.

8 **Establish priorities clearly, and link assessment to them.** For example, when an element of competence is broken down into six performance criteria, don't expect each criterion to be equally important. Use assess-ment details to show students which performances, and which pieces of evidence, to put their best efforts into.

9 **Use short print-runs!** After implementing the teaching and assessment of a competence framework just once, there will be a substantial number of adjustments you should expect to wish to make to it, based on experience. Don't become lumbered with large stocks of outdated documents.

10 **Don't pretend that because you've got a competence framework, assess-ment will be entirely objective.** Most competence frameworks simply mean that the decision-making tasks involved in assessment are smaller and more manageable, but they are still always subjective in the final analysis.

54

Assessing transferable skills

At a meeting, students were discussing their experiences of recent interviews. 'How did it go?' asked one. 'Not very well' came the reply. 'They asked me if I had developed any personal transferable skills as part of my course, and I didn't know what they meant.' 'Of course you have – you were Treasurer of the Canoe Club and you gave a presentation about your project...'. The following suggestions may help you – and your students – to address such skills.

1 **Open up a debate about what these skills are.** Different terminology abounds, from common skills, personal transferable skills, core skills and so on. The skills themselves normally include those relating to communication (written and verbal), working with others, numeracy, foreign languages, presentation, leadership, and adhering to values.

2 **Select which common skills to address in the context of your students' work.** Make sure that the skills are clearly relevant to the subject and topic, and not seen as optional extras by your students.

3 **Brainstorm with students the evidence they need to produce to prove their development of each skill.** Then open up a discussion about different levels of the respective skills, and how these levels may be distinguished by the quality and nature of the evidence.

4 **Collect examples of evidence of common skills for students themselves to assess.** Such evidence may take many forms, ranging from written reports to video-recorded interviews or presentations.

5 **Think about how the chosen skills can best be developed.** Before thinking about assessing such skills it is useful to think about where their development best fits into the course or module. A grid or matrix format may work well in planning which skills relate to which parts of a course. With modular programmes, it can become more complex deciding how to plot an individual student's development of a range of skills.

6 **Ask whether the skills are involved in all years of a course.** There is a tendency, for example, to think that presentation skills should be addressed in Year 1 and can then be ticked off. It is useful to think how such skills should be developing throughout a course, and how the levels should advance appropriately.

7 **Allow students the opportunity to use a range of media to demonstrate transferable skills.** Some skills can best be demonstrated with evidence derived from leisure activities, home life or work contexts. The evidence may comprise documents, tapes, videos, or computer programs. It is often valuable for students to include testimonials and statements of competence, provided by qualified colleagues, supervisors and others, who can testify appropriately to the achievements of the candidate.

8 **Get students involved in the assessment of others' competences.** Peer assessment of each other's transferable skills is an excellent method of enabling students to develop their own skills, and also provides a high level of engagement and commitment.

9 **Help students to develop their ability to evaluate their own transferable skills.** They can do so in a variety of ways such as filling in self-assessment forms, writing reflective accounts and participating in evaluative discussions or vivas with peers and/or tutors.

10 **Refer closely to the particular requirements of your own context.** For example, BTEC and GNVQ give very clear guidance about what is expected in the assessment of such skills, and many universities have their own strategies and policies on core skills or transferable skills, to which you should relate your own assessment methods.

Lessons From A Hammock

Much of this book was written during the memorably fine summer of 1995, at Brenda Smith's wonderful home in deepest Nottinghamshire, which boasts a lovely garden with a hammock. The following suggestions swung out of a synectics exercise conducted in and around the hammock!

1 **Assessment should be balanced.** Candidates should not have any surprises such as coming down to earth with a bump.

2 **Students should not be allowed to slip through the net.** The design of assessment systems should take into account the stature of the students.

3 **Assessors should not allow themselves to be easily swayed.** This can cause some dizziness, not to mention a lack of objectivity.

4 **There should be adequate arrangements for those who fall (fail).** When things go wrong, students need to be able to land softly and remain uninjured.

5 **Students should be well supported.** Assessment devices need to be suspended from stout pillars (of wisdom?).

6 **There should be equality of opportunity.** Students should not have to wait too long for their turn at assessment.

7 **The burden of assessment should not overstretch the system.** (Co-authors of books on assessment should not eat too many desserts!)

8 **Students should be protected from extraneous irritants during assessment.** Wasps, for example, should not be allowed to interfere with students' concentration.

9 **Disaster can occur with group assessment if the mass of the group becomes too large.** Some assessments can only be done one at a time.

10 **A helping hand (or foot) from a tutor may be needed to get assessment in motion.** Students can't always gain momentum on their own.

An Assessment Manifesto

We'd like to end this book by stating some values which we believe should underpin assessment, extending those which we outlined near the beginning. Our thinking on these values owes a debt to the work of the Open Learning Foundation Assessment Issues Group, in which we all participated, and to the values adopted by the Staff and Educational Development Association (SEDA) for its Teacher Accreditation Scheme, and Fellowship Scheme.

1 **Assessment should be based on an understanding of how students learn.** Assessment should play a positive role in the learning experiences of students.

2 **Assessment should accommodate individual differences in students.** A diverse range of assessment instruments and processes should be employed, so as not to disadvantage any particular individual or group of learners. Assessment processes and instruments should accommodate and encourage students to show creativity and originality.

3 **The purposes of assessment need to be clearly explained.** Staff, students, and the outside world need to be able to see why assessment is being used, and the rationale for choosing each individual form of assessment in its particular context.

4 **Assessment needs to be valid.** By this, we mean that assessment methods should be chosen which directly measure that which they are intended to measure.

5 **Assessment instruments and processes need to be reliable and consistent.** As far as is possible, subjectivity should be eliminated, and assessment should be carried out in ways where the grades or scores that students are awarded are independent of the assessor who happens to mark their work. External examiners and moderators should be active contributors to assessment, rather than observers.

6 **All assessment forms should allow students to receive feedback on their learning and their performance.** Assessment should be a developmental activity. There should be no hidden agendas in assessment, and we should be prepared to justify to students the grades or scores we award them, and to help them to work out how to improve. Even when summative forms of assessment are employed, students should be provided with feedback on their performance, and information to help them identify where their strengths and weaknesses are.

7 **Assessment should provide staff and students with opportunities to reflect on their practice and their learning.** Assessment instruments and processes should be the subject of continuous evaluation and adjustment. Monitoring the quality of assessment should be built in to quality control processes in universities and professional bodies.

8 **Assessment should be an integral component of course design, and not something bolted on afterwards.** Teaching and learning elements of each course should be designed in the full knowledge of the sorts of assessment students will encounter, and be designed to help them show the outcomes of their learning under favourable conditions.

9 **The amount of assessment should be appropriate.** Students' learning should not be impeded by an overload of assessment requirements, nor should the quality of the teaching conducted by staff be impaired by excessive burdens of assessment tasks.

10 **Assessment criteria need to be understandable, explicit and public.** Students need to be able to tell what is expected of them in each form of assessment they encounter. Assessment criteria also need to be understandable to employers, and others in the outside world.

Suggestions For Further Reading

We think it is inappropriate in a book of this sort to cross-reference our suggestions extensively to the work of other authors, and preferable to include a selection of those texts, pamphlets and articles on assessment and related issues which we think readers will find useful. We have also tried to cluster our suggestions for further reading around some of the principal themes of the current book.

General texts on assessment

Andressen, L, Nightingale, P, Boud, D and Magin, D (1989) *Strategies for Assessing Students – Teaching with Reduced Resources*, SEDA Paper 78, Birmingham, UK.

Angelo, T A and Cross, K P (1993) *Classroom Assessment Techniques* (2nd edition), Jossey-Bass, San Francisco.

Atkins, M J Beattie, J and Dockrell, W B (1993), *Assessment Issues in Higher Education*, Department of Employment, London.

Banta, T W, Lund, J P, Black, K E and Oblander, F W (1996) *Assessment in Practice*, Jossey-Bass, San Francisco.

Bell, C and Harris, D (1994*) Evaluating and Assessing for Learning* (2nd edition), Kogan Page, London.

Brown, G, Bull, J and Pendlebury (1997) *Assessing Student Learning in Higher Education*, Routledge, London.

Brown, S and Knight, P (1994) *Assessing Learners in Higher Education*, Kogan Page, London.

Brown, S and Race, P (1994) *Assess Your Own Teaching Quality*, Kogan Page, London.

Brown, S, Rust, C and Gibbs, G (1994) *Strategies for Diversifying Assessment in Higher Education*, Oxford Centre for Staff Development, Oxford Brookes University.

Brown, S and Smith B (1997) *Getting to Grips with Assessment*, SEDA Special No. 3, Birmingham, UK.

Cox, K R and Ewan, L E (1988) *The Medical Teacher*, Churchill Livingstone, Edinburgh.

Coulson, A (1994) *Objective Testing*, Red Guide Series 11, 4, University of Northumbria at Newcastle.

Crooks, T (1988), *Assessing Student Performance*, HERDSA Green Guides, 8, University of New South Wales, Australia.

Knight, P (ed) (1995) *Assessment for Learning in Higher Education*, Kogan Page SEDA Series, London.

Matthews, L (1994) *The Range of Marks in Assessment*, Red Guide Series 8, 4 University of Northumbria at Newcastle.

Matthews, L (1994) *Managing Dissertation Supervision*, Red Guide Series **8**, 5 University of Northumbria at Newcastle.

Miller, A H, Imrie, B W and Cox, K (1998) *Student Assessment in Higher Education , A Handbook for Assessing Performance*, Kogan Page, London.

Palomba, C A and Banta, T (1999) *Assessment Essentials – Planning, Implementing and Improving Assessment in Higher Education*, Jossey-Bass, San Francisco.

Race, P (1993) *Never Mind the Teaching, Feel the Learning*, SEDA Paper 80, Birmingham.

Race, P (1995) *The Art of Assessing: Part 1*, New Academic, **4**, 3, SEDA, Birmingham.

Race, P (1995\6) *The Art of Assessing: Part 2*, New Academic, **5**, 1, SEDA, Birmingham.

Rowntree D (1989) *Assessing Students: How Shall we Know Them?* (2nd edition), Kogan Page, London.

On Supplemental Instruction

Buckley, C (1993) *Supplemental Instruction*, Red Guide Series **8**, 2, University of Northumbria at Newcastle.

Rust, R and Wallace, J (1994) *Helping Students to Learn from Each Other*, SEDA Paper 86, Birmingham.

On Large Groups

Gibbs, G and Jenkins, A (1994) *Teaching Large Classes in Higher Education*, Kogan Page, London.

Gibbs, G (1992) *Assessing More Students*, Oxford Centre for Staff Development, Oxford Brookes University.

On Self- and Peer-Assessment

Baume, C and Baume D (1986) *Learner Know Thyself – Self-Assessment and Self-Determining Assessment in Education*, The New Era, **67**, 3, 5–67.

Brown, S and Dove, P (1991) *Self- and Peer-Assessment*, SEDA Paper 63, Birmingham.

Brown, S and Dove, P (1992) *Self- and Peer-Assessment: A Guide for Enterprising Students*, Red Guide Series 3, 1, University of Northumbria at Newcastle.

Boud, D and Lublin, J (1983) *Self-Assessment in Professional Education*, University of New South Wales, Australia.

Boud, D (1986) *Implementing Student Self-Assessment*, HERDSA Green Guides, **5**, University of New South Wales, Australia.

Boud, D (1992) The Use of Self-Assessment Schedules in Negotiated Learning, *Studies in Higher Education*, **17**, 2, 185–200.

Conway, R *et al* (1993) *Peer Assessment of an Individual's Contribution to a Group Project*, Assessment and Evaluation in Higher Education, **18**, 1, 45–56.

On Assessing Open Learning

Brown, S and Maher P (1992) *Using Portfolios for Assessment: A Guide for Enterprising Students*, Red Guide Series, **3**, 2, University of Northumbria at Newcastle.

Brown, S and Race, P (1995) *Assessing Open Learning*, Red Guide Series, **11**, 2, University of Northumbria at Newcastle.

Race, P (1992) *53 Interesting Ways to Write Open Learning Materials*, TES, Bristol.
Race, P (1994) *The Open Learning Handbook*, 2nd edition, Kogan Page, London.

On Assessing Competence and Transferable Skills

Brookes, J (1993) *A Cooperative Approach to the Development and Assessment of Skills in an Academic Programme*, Red Guide Series, **5**, 1, University of Northumbria at Newcastle.
Dobbins, M (1993) *Assessment of Work-based Learning*, Red Guide Series, **5**, 6, University of Northumbria at Newcastle.
Dove, P (1993) *NVQs: An Introductory Guide*, Red Guide Series, **5**, 3, University of Northumbria at Newcastle.
Edwards, A and Knight, P (eds) (1995) *Assessing Competence in Higher Education*, Kogan Page, London.
Fraser, W (1993) *Workplace-centred Integrative Assignments for Non-Placement Students*, Red Guide Series, **9**, 3, University of Northumbria at Newcastle.
Holmes, D and Reed, R H (1994) *Implementation and Assessment of Work-based Learning: A case study in biomedical sciences*, Red Guide Series, **5**, 4, University of Northumbria at Newcastle.
O'Hagan, C (ed) (1995) *Empowering Teachers and Learners through Technology*, SEDA Paper 90, Birmingham.
Rhodes, G (1993) *GNVQs: An Introductory Guide*, Red Guide Series **5**, 5, University of Northumbria at Newcastle.

On Learning Contracts

Anderon , G, Bond, D and Sampson, J (1996) *Learning Contracts – A Practical Guide*, Kogan Page, London.
Boak, G (1998) *A Complete Guide to Learning Contracts*, Gower, Hampshire, UK.
Brown, S and Baume, D (1992) *Learning Contracts, Vol 1: A Theoretical Perspective*, SEDA Paper 71, Birmingham.
Brown, S and Baume, D (1992) *Learning Contracts, Vol 2: Some Practical Examples*, SEDA Paper 72, Birmingham.

Useful addresses for some of the above publications

Oxford Centre for Staff Development, Oxford Brookes University, Headington, Oxford, OX3 0BP.
Red Guides: MARCET, Educational Development Service, University of Northumbria at Newcastle, Newcastle upon Tyne, NE1 8ST.
SEDA Publications (also HERDSA Publications in the UK): Gala House, 3 Raglan Road, Edgbaston, Birmingham, B5 7RA.

Index